# PREGNORANT

## LALANII ROCHELLE

FOR TYE'LER, MY HEARTBEAT

REMEMBER, EVEN WHEN IT BREAKS,

IT STILL BEATS.

I LOVE YOU,

YOUR MOM

Cover image by Casey Sklar of Hand Me Down Art

@_hand_me_down_

The names and identifying characteristics of some of the individuals featured throughout this book have been changed to protect their privacy.

Copyright ©2021 Lalanii Rochelle

All rights reserved.

No part of this publication may be reproduced, stored in retrieval system or transmitted in any form or by any means, electronic, mechanical, photocopying recording or otherwise, without the prior written permission of the publisher.

# TABLE OF CONTENTS

PREGNORANT ................................. 1

MONTH TWO: FLY .............................. 7

MONTH THREE: FOOD DIARY ..................... 36

MONTH FOUR: GROUND .......................... 89

MONTH FIVE: DOPPELGÄNGER .................... 117

MONTH SIX: SLEEPTALKING NAKED ............... 149

MONTH SEVEN: DADDY DOESN'T DANCE ............ 181

MONTH EIGHT: ABSENT PARENT QUESTIONNAIRE . 223

MONTH NINE: LABOR ........................... 275

EPILOGUE: THEY DON'T TELL YOU ............... 323

ACKNOWLEDGMENTS: ............................ 351

# PREGNORANT

Waiting—staring at the front steps for my mama to get home was like sitting in a diaper I'd shat in. Easy enough—I'd then explain to her I accidentally opted to change diapers for a few years, starting with my own. All I could think about was what she was going to say, think, do. She knew I was smarter than getting pregnant at fifteen. But I was *Pregnorant* at fifteen. My stomach bubbled.

Oh, I could just say I'd loved how horribly she drank wine and yelled all the time so clearly motherhood was so divine, that I'd indirectly chosen this path as my own. I *like* falling up stairs. I *love*

## PREGNORANT

failing wide if I'm gonna. Truth is? All the sarcasm and aeronautics I could float, fly, or climb weren't getting me out of this one. It felt easier to jump out of a plane in the sky—scared of heights. How does one trust the plan when the plan is so full of surprises?

\*

PREGNORANT

## **After But Before**

After I ran out of the abortion clinic at fifteen,

but before I learned pregnancies could happen without orgasms…

After I learned love doesn't always stick, but before I learned

children aren't traps for love that didn't last long enough

After and happenstances don't have happy dances, but before I

leave—better yet afterward,

Happiness isn't just in you—it's your state of mind and the

questions we ask ourselves

Surely there must be some kind of special disaster to make sure

before I knew better you would love me enough or more after this

## PREGNORANT

Before and for all Pregnorancies and Absentee Assholes ~ we just didn't know any better but to be to the limits of what we could dream but not highly sought after it

After it is all said and done, we made one helluva Heartbreak, not lowercase but capital... before I thought I knew more than I knew

After I thought my heart would just sink in, but before it actually did, there was a headstrong little kid looking up after me, hoping he could do as well as I didn't

But did... and before we all grew up to know our parents are just floating the boat best they can but after that—

PREGNORANT

I wish we'd all get our wings, after everything **they don't tell you**, but before it all loses meaning enough and he blames me for how well he didn't do yet

After I take all the guilt with me to cry over the milk I no longer drink—but before it spilt... I'll tell you the story of how it went... since I knew more after than before—when it made sense.

I was *Pregnorant.*

PREGNORANT

Here it goes... happy now?

## MONTH TWO:

## FLY

I'd always felt like I was thought of as the "smart one" of the family. The one who got teased about reading books, wearing nerdy glasses, and carrying different-colored pens. I could already hear the change:

"Book smarts ain't street smarts."

"Baby havin' baby."

Seraphs in my dreams had big fat wings; they floated—not flew. All 109 pounds of me and my curly brown hair could hardly move.

## MONTH TWO: FLY

My high cheekbones flushed. I've always had "pretend wings." I would wake up staring at the same squirrel-infested tree I went to sleep staring at. Most of those days I was so sick—even breathing was hard. And then there were those moments when vomit got stuck between throat and tongue, when I'd sometimes wonder if I'd slept at all. Where was I when asleep between waking? Were there, ever, even squirrels?

MONTH TWO: FLY

"and she says

when I defame her

dream:

you are trying to

pull me down

by the wings."

—Bukowski

## MONTH TWO: FLY

Mama arrived. She stood just under five feet as well, miniature dark almond cookie, brown hair, petite shape, can of Miller Lite at 10:07 on any morning. Definitely beer in hand this high-flying afternoon. "Did you call ya daddy and tell him you're ova here?" I shook my head no. She didn't know yet, and I would have traded stars for stop signs halting everything in my world not to have her disappointed. She had walloping wings that matched her ferocious personality—that and the way she usually accepted my flaws gave her wings: mulberry wings because purple was her favorite color and I love to "fancy-up" things.

"I'm pregnant." All the world cornered me. All I had was funneled vision and a jittery heartbeat—enough to make anyone not believe in anything anymore.

## MONTH TWO: FLY

"Well, what are we going to do?" Mama squinted. Listened. At any other moment she only heard me a third of the time. I sometimes thought she had only one fully working ear, and it was conveniently up for sale. But I was wrong; she'd heard me. Just when I'd thought her wings had been impounded, I saw them being restored. I saw them gently unfurling as she stared at my two-month pregnant belly button showing through my blouse.

Mama reacted with an eerie, high-pitched "ok baby, everything's fine" voice, leaving me uneasy and afraid she would backhand me for being so frivolous with my "treasure." When a woman from Baton Rouge, Louisiana, decided to get quiet, it meant she was planning her comeuppance, her reckoning. I would get her true reaction later. But the anger never came. I would've preferred it to

## MONTH TWO: FLY

the reality—embarrassment and embarrassment with a side of "you ain't gon' be nothin'. " Hole in my wing, nose dive.

I felt nothing but nausea. Usually at the onset, I'd talk to my little pea pod and hold my stomach tight. Something told me my baby would remain healthy if I talked to my belly often, so I did. Some crazy study would've proven me right. "Please don't make us sick, don't be mean," I'd say as nausea subsided. Moments later, that nausea would sneak back up on me like a vulture with black wings whose hooked nails would push down into my back, then spring me into flight. I'd topple over holding on tight to the side of any toilet, cry.

\*

## MONTH TWO: FLY

As my stomach tossed and turned, I thought about my family. My parents split after thirty years—what should have been their eternity collapsed in what seemed to me to have been just a few months before my pregnancy was discovered, but maybe it was years–ya know? I remember popping back and forth from house to house. I thought they were legally married, but when Dad took Ma to court for child support, I figured out they weren't. Dad, who'd made all the money for years and years, would go so low as the Superior Court. The court granted him sole custody and because he worked under the table, they ordered her to pay him. As I would soon find out, in an emotional storm, it's really hard to fly straight, most times.

Mama was trying to get money after having spent so many years with him. She had family members as witnesses inventing

## MONTH TWO: FLY

gargantuan lies. But to no avail. Daddy devised some elaborate scheme that required Mama to pay child support to him until I was eighteen. I still couldn't imagine what Ma must have felt like. I remember Dad confessing once that he hadn't wanted Mama to work, so even if her paying child support had been possible, it wouldn't have been possible. She didn't even know a "working woman's" plight. In other words, she wouldn't make the flight again after being grounded so many years.

What I'd later come to learn was they didn't marry because up until about a year or so after I was born, Dad was still legally married to someone else. Someone he divorced when I was a toddler, but even still—he didn't marry Mama. I don't think (at that time) Daddy loved her enough. Not loving someone enough sometimes makes you stay with a person for thirty years without

## MONTH TWO: FLY

officially marrying, while you wait for your feelings to sprout wings and grow in differently, I guess.

Daddy worked so hard—his wings went limp and listless. He realized early-on what he was good at wasn't exactly what would make him the most money, so he grew in *that*. He just wasn't very swift with it, so then came the all-nighters. Even though we all never really knew what *that* actually was, there were paint and supplies everywhere at the office, so—good enough. Sometimes, though, the perfectionist in him got in the way of "good enough."

Because my grades were consistently something to post on the refrigerator, Daddy expected me to move worlds with my language skills. He wanted me to be an attorney, maybe, since he often used to say stuff like, "Look at my little lawyer!" after any smart-aleck comment I'd make. He thought a few spelling competitions and a

## MONTH TWO: FLY

stint on my school's debate team were surely a good foreshadowing of how *my* wings would grow in.

Daddy could make a caricature better than anyone in this universe; he knew how to pull out every ridiculous detail. I wanted to write white puff clouds of poetry in the sky. The one thing I know? We both would love our art into the wee hours of the night. How did he expect me to clip my wings, really, if he never really clipped his—even if just a bit for balance?

Writing made me feel free—a form of escapism. Writing was flying, although my wings sometimes lacked that puff-cloud steam. I could never speak up for myself, but my words? My words worked like rocket ships in my clenched fists. I guess, now that I was pregnant, I wouldn't be speaking up, or flying. I'd be changing diapers in sleeplessness. No skywriting for me.

## MONTH TWO: FLY

Daddy owned one of the largest graphic design companies in Westwood for over thirty years. His daydreams became nightdreams; he'd married his work long before he failed to marry Mama. He made less and less time for his family. Mama needed a hobby. Instead, she hosted lavish parties at our beautiful home in downtown Culver City, complete with an open bar and "take-home plates"—all flying at Daddy's expense.

With Daddy an overworked graphic artist and Mama a conversationalist, it only made sense for me to become a writer. Daddy could make a cartoon live a whole new life on canvas in ten minutes. Before he started his business, he'd worked for big-name companies like Disney and Sony Pictures. When he drew, it was like he was flying. Instead, he chose commercial art: signs and

## MONTH TWO: FLY

banners. Typography. He flew the most exquisite calligraphy: freehand, each stroke in little sweeps, stunning streaks, no tracing.

Mama's best friend Helena looked like a pale yellow iguana. She was tall and lanky, her neck was long, and she had dark hair. I loved her for how giddy she made Mama but hated her for taking her out so often. Motherhood was a trap and your freedom. Motherhood was a strength and a weakness. Mama could be found regularly at the local lounge or club with Helena, creatively drinking herself out of her "almost-marriage." Mama cheated on Daddy with a married man. Her wings were repossessed.

Mama's married lover had a wife who was dying of cancer. I was maybe twelve when I started to get an idea about Mama's rendezvous, but I couldn't confirm anything. My business was to "get out of grown folks' business," as Mama would say, so I did

## MONTH TWO: FLY

just that. Was cheating on someone who didn't think you were good enough to marry any better if there were motives and explanations? Probably not. But Ma's lover had wings burdened by his cancerous wife. Ma had to help out.

Dad lost his ability to improvise—grief and shock swallowed him. He couldn't even provide basic work to those who ordered from his business, but he still pretended he was able to work. When I wrote stories and poems, I felt like I could catch the wind running. Which was just like *flying with your fear* 'cause you were still grounded but you could feel the wind. I fell in love with nonfiction around the same time Daddy couldn't believe his dumb luck. Mama could only deny everything: *Did you actually fly if no one saw you?*

I will always wonder what my life would have been like if she'd admitted to everything. Would they have reconciled? Would I have

## MONTH TWO: FLY

flown straighter… sooner? Would my dad have admitted to his hidden marriage? His rumored other children? The world he was so accustomed to escaping to? Would I have not flown into arms that could not hold me? Or was this the wayward pathway?

I'd never received a grade lower than an A except gym class—the idea of being forced to wear the same PE clothes for five days was too repulsive to endure. Tears would form warmly in my eyes without warning. I felt my wings shrivel smaller, surely unable to fly now, hardly able to stand. That black vulture might as well have handed me a walker with tennis balls on the bottom.

Walking around with invisible weights on now-invisible wings was like trying to quell the voices I never knew I could hear. Ma was busy trying to pretend it was ok that I was having a baby at fifteen. As days went on, I realized she didn't show anger because she felt

## MONTH TWO: FLY

sorry for me. Her silence shot more holes in my wings like a bird that forgot to take flight with his flock. Or maybe it was me who bored those holes. Every day, I got more pregnant; every day, I lost more dreams.

My whole body quivered like I'd been swimming in cold water. The next few days, we didn't say much until one day, as I looked up from my cereal, she said, "Well, it looks like we're gonna have a baby then, now, don't it?" Mama's face looked as though I'd broken her heart. But her voice told me she was supporting my decision. I couldn't smile, but I was happy. Her shimmery feathers continued to grow in, but at funereal pace. Those feathers were just as good as wings. They had to be.

Less than a week or so later, Mama began to add extra laundry to my load of helping out to show me what my responsibilities would

## MONTH TWO: FLY

be from now on. She called all of my tenth grade teachers, gossip gurus, and not-even-close family members to advise them that, "Lawwwd, my baby is havin' a baby." Just as I'd thought. I wished I could plug her mouth up like the nozzle-tube they had been planning to use when I'd been scheduled for an abortion. Must the world know I was having a child? Was this grandchild by her child her rite of passage? I could have spat on her wings now.

The news spread like a drug dealer selling crack from this town to the next. I'd cry because my body was conditioned to cry. I'd cry when I'd think of the sound of Henry's voice, my soon-to-be "baby daddy." Tears would slide down without warning as I'd run to the sink, bracing the basin to throw up oatmeal, raisins, and banana bread. Again, I cried. I cried for my wings and for the things I'd never see because I'd have to give my baby my wings.

## MONTH TWO: FLY

Feeling sorry for myself, I sobbed so hard when I pulled away from my pillow strands of slobber were still there. For every second I wished he wasn't missing, or wished he were witnessing, I cried for Henry. He was entertainment—the funniest, cockiest expression of genuine high school foolishness I'd ever—never should have—met. I'd cry for my virgin wings I wished I'd kept, or I wish he wouldn't have clipped, or I wish I wouldn't have slept in.

Henry always had the latest Jordan tennis shoe. If the shoe came out at 7:00 a.m. on a school day, by the time his crew reached school, Henry had already exchanged the laces for opposing colors and was showing them off like an overzealous peacock. We didn't go to the same school, but news like this everyone knew. Headstrong and narcissistic, he was my very first cup of good coffee, how I liked it, and with all attentions to detail. I loved

## MONTH TWO: FLY

confidence because I lacked confidence. We flew together, but in the end we just made a baby that neither of us were ready for.

His lively ways were side-splitting in the most absurdly original and artsy-punk-witted way, so much so that at times I thought he didn't make any sense; then I would get it and realize he was talented and overconfident of his craft—which was making me laugh. He'd tease me or imitate me, making me laugh at myself. His hugs were wings. He'd tickle me upside down in every spot he could find on me. It wasn't pretend to me. It was the first time I was really flying.

Henry's wings tingled. They were wide, high spirited, and impulsive. They were navy blue, had to be—it's the color he wore most. His black hair and smooth skin. His foolhardiness matched his swollen-headed shenanigans. Once, I jumped full speed onto

## MONTH TWO: FLY

him—piggyback style—and he caught me. Might as well have called it a hot air balloon ride, I was so high up.

He was my first real boyfriend, if they could be real at fifteen. Over a year's time we'd fallen into the most enchanted helium-filled loveliness. Aphrodite envied us. It was a winged love, beyond reality, floating. We used to talk on the phone nightly, even beyond our phone hours. When one of our parents would pick up to check if we were still on, we'd both hang up and often leave them on the line laughing at us.

When our wings touched, it was kismet—there was no mistaking how much we enjoyed each other. He'd never once forgotten to call and goodnight me, or ring and wake me. There were moments we thought we'd talked everything out, so we listened to each

## MONTH TWO: FLY

other breathe. Then came another flighty conversation. Maybe in another life we were aerialist partners.

Once Henry knew I was pregnant, he made himself scarce. I thought he'd at least call to check on me. I only heard of what he was doing through mutual friends. I'd developed cooties without being aware of it. He was dodging me, so I saved face by pretending I didn't care that he wasn't around. Some days, when I'd doze off I'd picture him waking me, his eyelashes so close to my face it ached. I hated to acknowledge my disappointment in not checking the condom was on tightly and didn't break. He was a love that eventually didn't have the nerve to look me in my face. Some wings.

I sat alone at school, eating fries covered in cheese. I ran to throw up, and as I cried against the stall I remembered I used to break my computer games just to get daddy to take me to CompUSA so we

## MONTH TWO: FLY

could spend time together. He had stories printed on his wings, paintings, history—the most grandiose wings I'd ever seen. He used to tell me he spoke five languages, but if he didn't visit the places often enough, he would lose his ability to remember them.

Over the next few weeks, I began to agonize about how I'd left Daddy at the abortion clinic. I went from what some would call a potential baby murderer to a prospective mother, from victimized to erratic, from manic to moping havoc in a matter of moments. I was no fairy and could not fly. I was ***Wish Proof***; it'd all started with being ***Pregnorant.*** I knew if I didn't keep trying to reach my daddy, I would soon be one of the languages he could not remember.

Since I stayed with Daddy after my parents split, he found out about my pregnancy first. He got the jump on advising me what to do. I agreed to abortion because I knew it was what he wanted. I

## MONTH TWO: FLY

didn't care or know what was best for me until I thought about what it'd be like to wish I had my baby. Being pregnant at fifteen is like being shoved off a plane without knowing if your parachute will work, or if you know how to work it, or if you have one attached at all. Being shoved is different from jumping, just as flying is different from falling.

Daddy was successful at what he did. His banners and designs appeared 3-D on any flat surface. Daddy said my writing was phenomenal and he knew I'd be "one of those big-time authors one day." But that was only after he discovered how much I loved to write. The thought painted my hopes bright turquoise, but perhaps because I didn't hear it enough, I chose to chase Henry. People acknowledged having a boyfriend, but writing poetry in my diary? Not so much. I hated I had to have a boyfriend to feel ok. Why

## MONTH TWO: FLY

couldn't I just be ok by myself? Where were those wings when I needed them? What good were wings anyway? They were just pillowcases.

Sometimes I wrote poetry, mostly about wings. Sometimes about falling short. Sometimes about hope. Dean Young wrote in April 1999, "my wings wet capes and not working." In June of that same year, six months before my baby was born, I scribbled these words in my diary: "My wings were dreams on carousels, my wings upset and not growing, my wings don't let me fly no-where, my wings accept they're not going."

After I didn't leave the clinic with him, gossips told me Daddy waited for me in his SUV earlier than my dismissal bell every day. I knew he would reschedule the abortion, so I snuck out of class early or went out through the side gate of my school. This went on

## MONTH TWO: FLY

for weeks while I went to Mama's house. I was supposed to get a new car for my grades that year, a white Toyota RAV4. Instead, I'd be getting a baby and learning to breastfeed. Daddy had lost his angel and now had to watch her wingless.

From Daddy's perspective, not only had I chosen to have a baby, but I had also chosen Mama over him. I'd run away to live with Mama with only my backpack. I'd planned to call him about the pregnancy and tell him I didn't choose Mama over him, but only clichéd explanations came to mind. I'd never thought of myself as an "it just happened" type of girl.

Having hope meant it was ok that sometimes I had no wings, which was equivalent to being grounded enough to find the right person to love, or better, discovering what it was that made me love myself enough to stop looking for wings in someone else.

## MONTH TWO: FLY

Mary Oliver wrote, "I want / To think again of dangerous and noble things / I want to be light and frolicsome / I want to be improbable beautiful and afraid of nothing / as though I had wings." I wanted that.

Henry started stealing because his parents stopped giving him money for the tennis shoes he loved so much. He studied stealing more than any class, possibly to get attention, or perhaps it was his way of coping with my pregnancy. Maybe he was stealing long before then and I had no idea because I didn't know him as well as I thought I did. He'd steal from the front table of any Macy's department store and sell the name-brand merchandise at half the cost. Somewhere there must have been wings, but he was flightless.

## MONTH TWO: FLY

Rumors were—he'd get so high, nothing mattered to him. I heard after I got pregnant, he robbed a department store while he was on crutches by running a car through the front window. He'd attempted to hobble out with his merchandise, but his wingman in the getaway car left him behind. He became a true jailbird.

I was afraid Henry wouldn't love me if I had our baby, but he didn't seem to love me from the second he found out I was pregnant, which meant it wasn't the love I thought it was anyway. That was killing me. If I gave my baby up for adoption, I knew someone else would get to raise my child, which would have killed me too—if him not loving me weren't enough. Since without Henry I felt dead inside anyway, there was no reason not to ~~try~~ fly.

My pregnancy was nearing the end of its second month, and I still hadn't heard from him. He didn't have wings. I was not his. When

## MONTH TWO: FLY

he'd said he loved me, it'd been a lie. His hugs weren't wings; his hugs were memories. I remembered Henry kissing the top of my lips, the corners, and then my chin—adrenaline rushed through my arms. When he'd said he loved me, it'd been a lie. Sometimes a dream is just a dream.


But this baby was mine. My. Mine.


My mom's best friend, my godmom, called me when she heard the news I was pregnant. She said she was pregnant with her daughter at the same time my mom was pregnant with me. Her angelgirl was born around the same time but lived only days. A few times, she'd slipped and referred to me as her daughter. I never corrected her, not once.

## MONTH TWO: FLY

My godmom's baby died in her crib from sudden infant death syndrome. I dreamt I was that baby. When I woke up, I called her and cried out to her, "Nanny-nanny, I don't know what to do. I don't know if I should have my baby. I'm not against abortion and I'm not for it. I don't want people to think I'm a killer. I don't want people to think I'm a whore."

She replied, "Baby, baby, baby… the man upstairs is going to love you no matter what you do."

I didn't care about a man upstairs or downstairs, if anything existed or didn't. All I knew was I could feel purpose inside of me. She continued by asking me if I felt I needed to have my baby and if I'd thought about how my life would be if I didn't. She was the only one to ask me how I felt—she was concerned—when everyone else thought I had hooker disease.

## MONTH TWO: FLY

That was enough for me to feel wind. Breathe. One day, I would get my wings. Images of her daughter—sleeping to death—played in my heart on repeat.

# MONTH THREE:

# FOOD DIARY

**Week One**

Day One: 6:24 a.m.

Weigh myself: 114 lbs. I'm exactly three months pregnant.

- *1 cup of milk. Grilled cheese. Hunger pangs. At least I slept through the night. It feels as though I am hungry all of the time.*

## MONTH THREE: FOOD DIARY

**M**y life up until two months ago was a tight-roped plan I could balance. Remember that aerialist I told you I was around Henry? No more.

- *I imagine it's a little vampire fighting with me for my raisins. Munch on Corn Pops without milk. Half a turkey sandwich. Gala apple. Falling asleep. Still managed to eat other half of sandwich.*

Mama gets on my nerves. One second she's as sweet as a yellow peach, next second she's screaming at me about cleaning something up, or she'll say, "Get off your lazy ass because shit's gon' change 'round here real soon!" I feel like a Tonka truck crawled inside of me and the engine died.

## MONTH THREE: FOOD DIARY

- *Four and a half eggs with ketchup, half piece of bacon, glass of OJ, plate of grits with syrup and jelly, two burnt biscuits because Mama forgot them in the oven. Another glass of OJ. Throw up. Cinnamon Toast Crunch—my favorite cereal. Sleep.*

I watch *ER*, and the crack girl's baby dies. I cry because I'm so fat and depressed I don't want to go to Homecoming. Nia calls and says she plans to go and so does Henry. She offers to make sure he's not with any other girls, but I just start crying. The phone keeps ringing, and I startle when the first word out of some girl's mouth is his name or, "Your baby daddy did this or that." I hear he's all over the place with everyone, and I'm stuck here busy growing a baby. I'm also busy hoping that I can wait until dinner is

## MONTH THREE: FOOD DIARY

ready because all that matters is what's for dinner and how long dinner is going to take to be ready.

- *Canned fruit cocktail. Red paradise-flavored Popsicle. Stomach growling. I answer back. I have asked my belly what he or she wants to eat and if he or she is sleepy. My body seems to be pulling me much like the way a child has a tantrum and the mother has to jerk and tussle with her little one. Cornish hens with gravy. Broccoli. Carrots. Macaroni n' cheese. Gas bubbles. Wrenching pain. Ginger ale soda. Sleep.*

Nightmare. When I wake, I trace dried tearstains along my face.

MONTH THREE: FOOD DIARY

Day Two: 3:08 a.m.

My eyes flutter open like I haven't slept the entire night. While sleeping, I flash back to Henry and I kissing in the doorway. Behind us is a long green hallway.

- *Cinnamon Toast Crunch cereal. Spit milk back in bowl. Throw up. Still hungry. Gala apple. Turkey sandwich, mayo stinks.*

*Sleep 1:30 p.m.– 6:30 p.m. Wake up tired.*

- *Potatoes with ketchup and barbeque sauce. McDonald's chicken sandwich with hot mustard sauce. Salty fries.*

MONTH THREE: FOOD DIARY

There are no messages on the machine, and my pager isn't lighting up. I've lost track of whether it's morning, afternoon, or time for another nightmare.

- *Craving for bubbles. Soda. Feel like I need to burp for hours but can't.*

Day Three: 7:00 a.m.

- *Cinnamon Toast Crunch. Again.*

I have a 9:00 a.m. appointment with Dr. Kavin. Doc says no more sugar, no more salt, no more fried foods or candy. That's everything I eat. How am I going to do this?

- *Diet Mountain Dew soda. Water. Turkey sandwich.*

## MONTH THREE: FOOD DIARY

If I lie on my back with my eyes open, it feels unnatural to sleep. If I lie on my side, I have to switch every twenty minutes because my neck feels stiff. If I lie on my stomach, I feel like I'll be hurting the baby. My elbow slips off the kitchen table and I nearly hit my chin. I'm starving in a figure eight of hunger that goes on and on and on.

- *Cinnamon honey graham crackers. Milk.*

Mama tells me drinking milk while pregnant will create varicose veins. I vow no more milk. Blue veins bulging out would look nasty.

- *Gala apple. Salad. Boiled egg.*

Hungrier than a mountain bear on steroids. I speak to Henry! We get along. Not how we used to laugh and sit on the telephone talking about nothing, but on some humane level, we get along.

MONTH THREE: FOOD DIARY

His tone toward me is different. Read in a magazine that the average labor is equivalent to jogging twelve miles. I tire walking down to the car to get Mama's beer cooler for her.

- *Cucumbers. Piece of pizza. Screw the doctor—this pizza is my doctor. Mashed potatoes, green peas, and creamed corn.*

Don't know what Ma made as meat, but whatever it is, baby me doesn't want it. Or want to smell it.

Day Four: 7:03 a.m.

- *Bagel with cream cheese. BLT. Bacon doesn't go over so well.*

## MONTH THREE: FOOD DIARY

Wake around 5:00 p.m. because I get a call from Henry's mother, Shiree, inquiring about my blood type, and she mentions twins are on her side of the family. This is the only time she's called since news of the cataclysm. Her screeching, condescending tone stings my ears even though I know her intention is to be cordial. Her universe keeps turning as usual. It keeps replaying in my head that she works at a college. Because of this, I wonder: *Shouldn't she be required to have more people skills?* She goes on about how she hopes her son's child will be a girl. I called the house a few times before her call—searching for Henry—and it seemed like she was full of excuses for where he was and when he'd get back to me. He never did. Shiree wants me to abort my pregnancy, and there is no way she can pretend to be excited.

- *Two slices of pizza. Salad, beans, some meat that makes me feel sicker. Throw up. Sleep.*

MONTH THREE: FOOD DIARY

Day Five: 4:03 a.m.

I wake from another nightmare of me in a wheelchair, unable to move or have any more children. My heartbeat like a wrecking ball coming for my collarbone. Today would've been Henry and I's sixteen-month anniversary.

- *Cinnamon raisin butter bread. Apple Jacks. 2% milk. Throw up. Hot dog with mustard and ketchup.*

Mama hasn't gone shopping yet. Ever cried while stuffing a hot dog in your mouth as you stare in the mirror?

I look down the hole in the sink as I throw up, and I fear that down that hole is where I will be for the rest of my life. In this moment, I

## MONTH THREE: FOOD DIARY

finally understand why having this baby isn't a great idea. This is a baby I will raise alone. Not by choice. Throw up in heaves.

- *Ate turkey sandwich. Hate the mayo from school cafeteria.*

Belly button feels hard inside; it's an "outtie," so that feels weird. My wonderful stretch pants are feeling less stretchy today. Breasts are so tender hugs would hurt, but no one is hugging me. I don't want them to.

- *Water bottle. Dizzy. Throw up.*

I cannot wait to go to another school. Here, everyone is staring at me, whispering about me, thinking about me, and pretending to be friendly. Henry pages me at 11:35 a.m. I figure he's paging

## MONTH THREE: FOOD DIARY

because he misses me terribly, and he's going to come to his senses and confess he will love me forever and the rest will be fairytale, but he's actually paging me because he's looking for his friend. Before I was pregnant, we celebrated cutesy one-month anniversaries from last spring to this spring, and now, now that I'm swelled with his baby, he decides not to acknowledge our Happy Anniversary today. How about that hug?

Day Six: 7:04 a.m.

- *Leftover teriyaki chicken for breakfast. Licorice. Nausea. Small OJ. Feel woozy. Fries with a little salt. Chicken fingers with no sauce.*

At school, I hear my name and "fat ass" in the same sentence. It seems everyone is smiling in my fat face and then later declaring

## MONTH THREE: FOOD DIARY

how fat I look. The last few times I've spoken to Henry, he seems to have developed a slight stutter, much like his father. I've never noticed it before, yet then again the relationship we had before was nothing like the nothing we have now. I miss my daddy.

Day Seven: 9:04 a.m.

- *Coco's Restaurant and Bakery: cinnamon French toast swirls with little syrup (trying to cut down on the sugar).*

I think about Daddy and Henry at breakfast. A newborn sits in her car seat in the booth next to ours. Mari and her mom take me to the restaurant. Mari is my dark-haired friend who was a cheerleader for Culver High School; I envied her because she was on the squad when I only made a drill team for a nearby park. She seems gleeful and excited for my pregnancy. Her mother's long black hair falls

## MONTH THREE: FOOD DIARY

against her face and she looks like some black shadow witch, but she speaks softly. I can see her thoughts, just like I can see everyone else's. They go something like, "She's so young, this will ruin her life, she thinks she knows what decision she's making, but she doesn't. Young and dumb, can't tell her anything." The baby cries out loudly, and it's as if I've never heard one cry. It's as if I'm trying to hear through *that* child what my child's cry will be.

**Week Two**

Day Eight: 3:02 a.m.

I wake up from a recount of whispers and am sweating all over. I'm thirsty but can't stop spitting. I drink half of a water bottle, and I leave my twin-size zebra-print bed and run to Mama's leopard-

## MONTH THREE: FOOD DIARY

print king-size bed. Ma's face buckles when she feels me slide in next to her. "What's wrong?" she whispers overexcitedly. I am at a loss for words and just look at her. She collects porcelain frogs, tiny frogs, oversized statuesque frogs, plastic frogs, and adorable African dwarf frogs in fish tanks—any possible type of frog. I can't understand because they are so repulsive. In the dark, she whispers to me that her love for frogs isn't based on physical attributes but on the fact that "frogs always jump forward, honey. When have you ever seen a frog jump backward?"

- *Baked biscuits. Two eggs. Then another of both.*

Toss and turn then force myself up. As I prepare for school, I drag my feet along the wood floor, plop down on the seat. I stare down at my belly, whispering to it.

MONTH THREE: FOOD DIARY

- *Two sausage links with mustard and ketchup. Two pieces of a green apple. All together. It tastes odd.*

I leave the apple on the counter to brown. Mama comes in fussing about the apple and the sink being stopped up. I was unaware that the sink wasn't a garbage disposal for my stomach rejections. She says the bathroom is a whole new type of disgusting.

- *Two pieces of cinnamon bread. Choke on it. Get an adrenaline rush while coughing.*

Day Nine: 2:22 a.m.

Sharp pain in abdomen. Wake in blistering pain. My pee is stinky. It feels like smoke is coming up from my stream of pee. It's a darker orange than usual. That's never been cause for alarm until

## MONTH THREE: FOOD DIARY

now, but then again, I've never had sex or been pregnant before. What if I have an STD? God. What if it's one that isn't curable and I'm stuck with it forever? What if I give a disease to my baby? I am in so much trouble. I should bury myself. I sit in silence, trying to figure out the right words for, "I need to go to the hospital because I am not ok in my vagina." I say nothing.

- *Doritos. Sprite. Chow mein. Salad. V8 Splash. Four raisins. Hard-boiled egg. A third of a cinnamon bun. Piece of chicken.*

Decide not to drink anything since the only time I feel the pain is when I have to use the bathroom. Ringing sting of pee sizzles as I squinch my whole body together. I pee and moan as it burns down my inner thigh. I holler out loud. Ma must be asleep already. She will think I am a complete whore. Not only did I go out and get

## MONTH THREE: FOOD DIARY

myself pregnant first wham, but I have now contracted heptavidavidavosis—what my father used to call illnesses I'd contracted from god-knows-where on the schoolyard when he didn't want to be around my sniffle or cough. Now I actually have a stinking, burning "cookie" filled with heptavidadvidavosis. The "cookie" was what Ma used to call my hairless princess vagina, when I would twirl around, sleeptalking naked like a princess after she'd lifted me from the bath, grabbing me with an oversized towel. I would snuggle in it and exclaim, "My cookie is clean, Mammi! My cookie is clean!"

Drink V8 down hard. I gulp and it hurts. I cry so hard I shake. I cry so much harder that I cry into a deep sleep. When I finally wake, I am fully clothed and my body is peeing on itself. I have a spoiled cookie now.

## MONTH THREE: FOOD DIARY

- *Chicken broth.*

Day Ten: 11:30 a.m.

Henry shows up at school and creates a buzz as everyone who knows of my pregnancy begins chanting, "Yo baby-daddie is herrrrrrreeee!" I curse the day I met Henry. My pee stings every time I use the bathroom. I make it the fastest process I can. Everyone is zizzing with excitement, declaring Henry nonchalantly announced to my sophomore class that I've been an "easy-hoe-bitch" and the kid I am carrying can't possibly be his.

Love might have made Henry remember that today was my sixteenth birthday. He never says hi.

- *I didn't eat at all.*

MONTH THREE: FOOD DIARY

Day Eleven: 8:00 a.m.

I'm supposed to go to school today, but instead I land at the WIC office (the Women, Infants, and Children's center), and I can hardly walk. The WIC office is another program for single low-income mothers, similar to AFDC (Aid to Families with Dependent Children), AFDC being another office Mama says I'd be in line for soon enough, as she can't keep up with the bills and makes too little to support me and my growing appetite. She works in escrow but always complains she's only an assistant and that "it don't pay for you and yo baby eatin' me outta house n' home." I think about the way Henry's wavy hair curls and shines atop his scalp. I wonder: If I killed myself and the baby, would he care about me then? As soon as I get home, I eat.

## MONTH THREE: FOOD DIARY

- *Potatoes, baked not fried. Barbeque sauce mixed with ketchup. Capri Sun. El Pollo Loco chicken drumstick. Mashed potatoes leftover on countertop. Half raspberry Popsicle. Six spoonfuls of broccoli out of the Tupperware. Tostitos with melted cheese. Everything I can smell or see in the refrigerator, on the table, or in the cabinets. Throw up and begin to sweat.*

I take an oversized swig of Pepto Bismol. I quickly remember I am pregnant and don't know what medicine will do to my baby. I spit it all over and fall to my knees, heart racing. I stare at the pink pool of mess as I shake, my head facing the floor.

- *Cereal. Banana. All I can think of is my cookie pain is killing me.*

## MONTH THREE: FOOD DIARY

After what Mama calls dramatics, she "drops my ass off back at school." I moan about it, but Mama reminds me again, "You wanted ta do this now, go'on 'head on,'" in her Southern accent that makes me never want any part of Louisiana. Her tone is always nonchalant but jarring. Oftentimes heartless—to make me really know she means it.

I watch my fat thighs jiggle down the hall to the office for my late slip, and I stare down at my bulging roll of a stomach. Then I stare down the hall.

It is just in time to see Henry make his grandiose appearance at my school again. He has his arms around two girls at the same time. He passes like he is a celebrity. Did he ditch, or was he even still enrolled? After I walk along in front of him, he makes way to turn himself, not releasing either of the girls (one I recognize because of

## MONTH THREE: FOOD DIARY

her big lips) to look at me as if to say, "Look what you can't have because you got pregnant." One of the girls is Amiah, and the other girl is cocking her head back like he's said something that tickled her. There's something to be said about a man who can make a girl laugh. I want to poke pencils into their eyes at the same time, those girls. I want to jab at Henry until he hits me back, until he fights me and fights me like he would fight a guy who just slept with his best friend. Until he fights me and fights me until he starts to fight *for* me. He just smiles haughtily at me and says nothing. I snarl on the inside and look away.

- *Dry salad from school cafeteria because I figure it'll be good for the baby.*

I call the doctor the second I get home because my cookie is still burning. The receptionist tells me to come in tomorrow because

## MONTH THREE: FOOD DIARY

my doctor isn't in on Wednesdays. What am I going to tell my mom? I cry in between peeing. Don't they know this is an emergency?

Day Twelve: 7:10 a.m.

- *Apple Jacks and 2% milk.*

Burning piss. Put headphones to my stomach for the first time. Swear I feel motion, but in the books I've read, three months is too early to feel anything. Gas bubbles. Must be gas.

- *Orange juice.*

Pee burns so bad my leg shakes.

- *Sweet Tarts.*

## MONTH THREE: FOOD DIARY

The 9:00 a.m. appointment waiting room is filled with babies and two big fat pregnant ladies. I can't believe I was judging big fat pregnant ladies when I'd soon be a big fat pregnant girl myself. After the receptionist calls my name, I glance back as my mom shakes her head. I scoot behind the big brown wooden doors to the room where they take my weight, then to the examination room. It is the fastest I've moved in days. I explained to the doctor my symptoms exactly. He takes notes and *hmm*s. He already knows my sexual history was nonexistent until now. He asks if I've been drinking much water, and I tell him no, but I have been drinking a lot of Capri Sun juices, milk, and orange and apple juices—all healthy for my baby. He asks me to meet him in his office without saying anything else. By the time I walk down the forever hallway and sit in the black leather chair, he's already writing a prescription. As he scribbles it out, he says to me, "You have

## MONTH THREE: FOOD DIARY

what's called a urinary tract infection, otherwise known as a bladder infection. Often women get these infections from their lack of water intake, or somehow bacteria reaches areas inside of the body where it doesn't belong. Mainly you'll need to drink more water and do your best to flush your body of toxins. Pure cranberry juice should help. No sugar."

I nod and say, "Ok." I guzzle a water bottle in the car and start to feel better instantly.

- *Ten glasses of lukewarm water.*

Mom asks me what the doctor said, and I shrug and repeat to her, "Just a lil' bladder infection is all." I tell her as if I'd known what such a thing was before ten minutes ago. Seeing my prescription in hand, she's already on her way to the pharmacy.

## MONTH THREE: FOOD DIARY

- *Cranberry juice cocktail from the lobby fridge outside of the pharmacy. Clam chowder. Water. Bloated. Spicy spaghetti from some hole-in-the-wall.*

Stop at Ross for my first pair of maternity pants. They are so hideously high on my waist. Mom laughs as she tells me it is only going to get better. I nearly faint.

- *Seven maraschino cherries from inside of the refrigerator door when Ma isn't looking.*

Maybe "little me" is a vegetarian? Fall asleep still hungry.

Day Fourteen: 7:37 a.m.

- *Cinnamon Toast Crunch.*

## MONTH THREE: FOOD DIARY

I feel like I'm going to die of boredom, loneliness, and hopelessness. Before I can bother with death, I see a commercial with a pretty girl with long black hair, swimming in a cool turquoise pool. I love that pools are a turquoise clear. I start to think of what my daughter or son will look like. I've always loved water.

- *Popsicle.*

I walk down to the pool with my dark shades, wearing a two-piece that is clearly too small for me. It's the first time I've seen my reflection, and I am pale and plump in the belly. I've never had a plump tummy! I am a "two-piece wearin' woman!" I love to run around in my panties and bra sets from the Fedco department store. Now, I'm ashamed of my midsection.

## MONTH THREE: FOOD DIARY

It is warm, just about hot. I swim for fifteen minutes, huff, and get out. Although it is refreshing, I am so lonely. I think about how Daddy isn't answering any of my calls and how I call daily and it just rings in the same unanswering way it does when I call Henry, who doesn't call back. I think about the look on my dad's face as he sat in the clinic.

- *Steak with sauce. Throw up.*

I burn badly. The look haunts me.

- *Water. Tears. Water. Tears.*

Sleep hard. Late in the night, I tiptoe to the bathroom to throw up swirls of a smelly, creamy-white substance. Baby didn't like the medicine I'd taken at all.

## MONTH THREE: FOOD DIARY

I finally get used to throwing up when pain shoots through my left leg. I moan loudly. Mama rushes to my side as I kneel by the toilet gripping the crevices in the tile floor. She puts her head on my shoulder and closes her eyes, much like the baby I'd seen on a bus once do to her mother.

**Week Three**

Day Fifteen: 10:13 a.m.

Wake up. Head pounding. Swallowing is hard. Ma yelling. Forgot to ask the doc for my proof of pregnancy paper to give to the WIC office. Don't give a flying stick about a pregnancy paper on this morning. On this morning, my throat is sore, my left ear is aching, and just when I thought waking up to boredom yesterday was bad,

## MONTH THREE: FOOD DIARY

I renege—waking up feeling in the mood to die is much worse. Mama says she'll make me the homemade kind of chicken soup later when she gets off work. She tells me my immune system must be a little bit weak. Ya think?

- *Warm canned chicken noodle soup.*

Scared to take any medicine, I sleep and weep quietly. I blow my nose, and I remember someone. Beatrice. Beatrice was my mother's longtime friend who lived in the back house of the property my father owned when I was growing up. She had terrible allergies. So bad I don't remember a time when her pale off-yellow skin tone wasn't pink, sore, and scabbed around the nose.

Try to drink water as I remember. The house I grew up in was surrounded with bushes, gladiolas, and exotic flowers of pink,

## MONTH THREE: FOOD DIARY

peach, and orange. My house was the front house. Beatrice lived in the one-bedroom behind us. My daddy owned it as well.

- *Saltines.*

I blow my nose. Beatrice met Kaden, an endless enticing Babyface Edmonds look-alike, and fell in overpowering love. He came around sometimes, but mostly it seemed around nightfall. By the time we all got to know of his presence, Beatrice was knocked up three or so months and heavily suffering with her allergies.

- *Sniffle. Apple.*

Beatrice was scheduled for a nose surgery that might've improved her allergies before she was told she was pregnant. Beatrice ignored medicinal warnings and continued with Benadryl

## MONTH THREE: FOOD DIARY

throughout her entire pregnancy, and her child was born with an enlarged, lopsided head.

- *Water. I examine the Tylenol bottle, holding it for a few seconds, and then I put it back in the cabinet and hold the cabinet closed.*

Beatrice's son, Isaac, was the only child I knew of who was handicapped. I often stared because I didn't know what else to do; it was like what I imagine looking at bodies being pulled from a three-car pile-up. I'd be mortified, but I wouldn't stop looking.

- *Water. Tissue, moaning.*

Kaden came around less and less, and Beatrice was soon raising her overdose mistake alone. She spoke so kindly and properly. At

## MONTH THREE: FOOD DIARY

five years old, Isaac still wore diapers and a helmet, and he rocked back and forth incessantly. Beatrice stopped paying her rent in return for our pity of her misfortune, and Daddy became more stressed than ever. I stuff my face with a piece of Hawaiian bread. Sniffle.

- *Water, pain, applesauce.*

I realize how much I miss living with my dad. Mama takes me by Daddy's to grab some of my old clothes, and as I walk up the curved sidewalk, I think about running into his room for a hug—I turn the lock in the key and it stops. It is stuck. I try the other keys, and they all stick as well. I go slowly through each key as I call for my mom. She tries every key with me one by one. But it is true. With my palm to the security gate, I bang the door. My other hand

## MONTH THREE: FOOD DIARY

is still struggling with the key as I refuse to accept the locks have been changed. My body runs out of tears that day.

- *Mom force-feeds me chicken soup.*

I mope myself to sleep, head banging with ache, and think I should have stayed out of the pool. I have regret for everything. Germs. It must have been germs in the pool. Today is Father's Day, and my father changed the locks on me. I almost throw up, then it sits in the back of my throat.

Day Sixteen: 12:04 p.m.

- *Bagel with cream cheese. Sporadic prenatal multivitamin to an upset stomach. Apple juice. Water. Water. Water. Baked potato.*

## MONTH THREE: FOOD DIARY

I begin to think about Henry's behavior—the way I keep hearing about him stealing name-brand merchandise scurrying off in Ashley's cream-colored Cadillac-like car. Thinking about the way I heard he'd gotten "put on"—which was colloquial for "accepted into"—one of L.A.'s largest gangs: the Rollin' Sixties. Thinking about the way I've heard the stories of other girls he is now "going with," which was what we called "courtship." Thinking about the way he dodged telling his parents I was pregnant the night I called to give everyone the news.

- *Several glasses of cranberry juice and water.*

I am thinking about why I am having my child, and I decide to eat one healthy thing for every solid reason I can find, and for every reason I feel I can't figure out, I decide I can eat something sweet or some form of junk food. Against any good sense, I carry this out:

## MONTH THREE: FOOD DIARY

*1. Because I love him. Vegetable soup.*

*2. Because I'm already tainted by losing my virginity anyway. Snickers.*

*3. Because he doesn't love me, and not having his laughter means I can hang on to his baby to give me joy. Broken candy cane.*

*4. Because I can't bear to look myself in the mirror. Cheese stick.*

*5. Because what if I get an abortion, and then I can't have children anymore? Seven Sweet Tarts.*

*6. Because Henry doesn't love me, and he might love me again if we have a baby together. Cinnamon bread.*

## MONTH THREE: FOOD DIARY

7. *Because he won't even call to see about how I'm doing, and this was one way, if not the only way at this point, to never ever let him go. The rest of the whole damn lemon cake that was half-stale in the fridge.*

8. *Because I can come through this like a fighter, but I just don't want to. Half a cup of OJ, one prenatal pill.*

9. *Because his mom is such a super amped up-bitch, and because she urged me to get an abortion in the first place. Chocolate syrup all-inner-swirling in my mouth.*

10. *Because I love him. Throw up and get the shits.*

Sleep. Wake in a nightmare of Henry's family trying to take custody of my son. My son! He's a boy. My child is a boy, I just

## MONTH THREE: FOOD DIARY

know it. Nightmare flashes to Henry bringing another woman to my baby shower. I smash cake into her eyes. Picture blurs to me holding my belly in pain as I scream unnatural things and my cousin Roxanne tries to hold me back.

- *A sandwich, salad with fat-free dressing. Lucky Charms. Carrots. Ginger ale. Nightly upchuck of red and green. Must it be Christmas already?*

I want to run away to a faraway land far away from far away. Henry's family members have red eyes and red teeth and are devils in my nightmare. Their hair is dark gold. The nightmare flashes to Henry in a green hallway, again another green hallway, and I can hear him but I cannot see anything but his red eyes. I wake and throw up water.

## MONTH THREE: FOOD DIARY

Day Seventeen: 11:00 a.m.

- *Raisin Bran. Flavored sparkling water. Banana. Slice of watermelon. Popsicle. Saltine crackers. Subway sandwich.*

Middle-of-the-night realization that I may never get married because if Henry doesn't want me, no one is going to want me after I have a baby already. No disrespect to young parents, but if I had to choose between experiencing love and making a baby, I would easily go without the baggage children usually bring. Maybe I should have gotten the abortion. It would have been over with by now. My life would be back to normal.

Normal. If normal is Daddy coming home at three in the morning every night busy working or making work a cop-out for the

## MONTH THREE: FOOD DIARY

responsibility he doesn't want. Or if normal is Mama going out to the Town House nightclub, slithering in like a skunk-funked snake who bathed in Crown Royal. Normal? Perhaps if normal is latchkey as lonely as a diary can make you. Yes, my life will go back to normal. But maybe normal is my own normal. Maybe normal is me—creating my own path and my own life with my own child. Maybe normal is accepting this responsibility and pushing forward, creating a new and better life for myself, created by myself. Or maybe that's all shit and I'm just afraid to have a vacuum suck up my baby.

- *Spicy spaghetti. Garlic bread.*

Do nothing today. Stay at Tia's in Rialto. Nice change of scenery. I want my own bed again. Or maybe I just want my own. My own person. My own amazing little piece of this world. Me. My. Mine. Now, all I yearn for is my own selfhood, not necessarily a baby but

## MONTH THREE: FOOD DIARY

my own individuality. My own stuff. My own voice. My own choices. Maybe once I'm a mother, when I say something people will respect and listen to me. My space. My life. Mine. My.

### Week Four

Whatever day, wake at 8:00 a.m.

I forget about writing in this diary and go out to marvel at wondrous things. A butterfly admiring the marigolds, delicious sunlight peering over dusty parked cars, causing shade for me… enough shade for me to sit wide-legged on the curb and get giddy when it takes me a few seconds longer than usual to get back up. Daily, I start walking around Ma's condominium with my Walkman on. Nightly, I let my baby hear too because they say

## MONTH THREE: FOOD DIARY

babies can hear in the womb. I play Mariah Carey because she's one of my favorites. I can't remember what I eat.

He has to be a he because in all of my wildly vivid dreams, he is tiny and the color of pale yellow clay. His name will be Dylan or Tyler. If he happens to be a girl, he will go nameless because I am that sure he is a boy. His middle name will be Julian, after Daddy.

- *Water. Doughnut—it tastes like a crayon. I remember chewing the tips of crayons as a child, so I know.*

Reminisce about Henry and me going to Disneyland, and the entire time we could not stop being extremely loving to each other. Craving cotton candy, but I don't have anyone to drive me to get some. Days are longer. Last week, I spoke to Henry for hours, and he reminded me what I'd fallen in love with. We are going to make

## MONTH THREE: FOOD DIARY

it as a family, and for this I feel so thankful and so proud! I knew I shouldn't have given up hope.

- *Strawberries! Why did I bother doubting? A whole bowl full of sugar-covered strawberries!*

Saw *Wild Wild West* featuring Will Smith with my old friend Esther and her on-and-off boyfriend, Jonathan. Esther is a Mel B. from Spice Girls look-alike. Esther and I were better friends a year ago when it was only fashion and boys to worry about. Now my heart is taken by my pregnancy and I am a third wheel on a date with her Justin Timberlake-ish guy who drives a white Bronco truck. She only wants him for his car.

- *Ate three meals each day. I kept them all down. Drank lots of water. Happy.*

## MONTH THREE: FOOD DIARY

Week four, whatever a few days later, wake 8:01 a.m.

- *Breakfast sandwich. Pineapples and prunes.*

I've been constipated lately.

- *Leftover fries for lunch. Chicken and green onions with honey barbeque sauce.*

Why honey barbeque sauce? Because I'm in a great mood and I am happy happy, happy to be alive and in this space. I slept well but woke up more than usual to use the bathroom.

A few days later, wake 8:02 a.m.

I'm getting the hang of this, I'm waking at regular times and not spending the day moping around. My spirit feels like it used to

## MONTH THREE: FOOD DIARY

before I got pregnant. I call Henry to make sure he'll be on time for the appointment **that** morning—like we'd talked about—and I hear a girl in the background.

- *Cheese balls. Chili dog. Doughnuts. Doughnuts. A whole pack of Red Vines. All of the Hershey's Kisses from Mama's glove compartment and a whole soda even though it's against my religion!*

Sobbing hysterically.

Maybe soda isn't against my religion, but you get it.

## MONTH THREE: FOOD DIARY

I go to my checkup alone. Tears ooze steadily down my face. After a few minutes, the doctor, nurse, receptionist, waiting room patients, and even my mother ask me if I am ok. I nod. Sip water bottle. Shake slightly.

At the checkup, the doctor says the baby's heartbeat is fast and strong.

- *Ate chips. Stomach growled.*

Of course it's today that Nia calls with the rumors of Henry sleeping with Amiah. Amiah used to be in a crew I would hang out with often; Nia is my very good friend from elementary school. Amiah had big fat lips, wavy sandy-brown hair, and beige-olive smooth skin. Nia reminds me of Foxy Brown and Kelly Rowland put together, she is headstrong and wears her hair short. She used

## MONTH THREE: FOOD DIARY

to style my hair when I could hardly brush through it once it got longer than my shoulders. Amiah is the little fuckerninny who was walking with Henry the other day at school.

- *Peanut Butter Crunch cereal. Chomped hard.*

The one time Amiah came to my house, Daddy couldn't stand her. When we ordered Thai food, Amiah spit the chicken back onto her plate in front of everyone at the table exclaiming, "Too hot!" No one could finish their food because we were all staring at the spit sparkling atop the piece of chicken. She was well over fourteen at this time. I lose my appetite when I think of Henry with her, hanging out after school at the Teen Center.

- *Appetite, appetite, where are you?*

## MONTH THREE: FOOD DIARY

Nia calls to update me later, informing me it was not only Amiah but potentially Stephanie as well. She gushes that she'd heard Henry was coming out of a popular apartment condo called Tara Hills, not too far from my own, a bit deeper into Culver City. Henry was allegedly there with his homeboy Ashley. Stephanie was with them, along with another girl who everyone knew Ashley liked for some time.

- *Took a gentle chocolate laxative for constipation.*

It is not gentle. Read more of my pregnancy book. Write nothing in my poetry journal; I just hold it close to me.

Week four, whatever who cares what day it is or what I ate, wake 11:00 a.m.

## MONTH THREE: FOOD DIARY

Eyes pop open this morning in fear of labor. I am not going to school today or caring about it. Mama doesn't wake me. I run around the house for the latter part of the day in my panties and bra again. I can see the way my stomach has grown, and it looks like it would look if I had eaten too much—yet all the time! It startles me sometimes when I accidentally run my hand over it.

- *French toast.*

Mama comes to get me on her lunch and takes the rest of the day off to take me to my AFP test at the doctor. I'm afraid, but the alpha-fetoprotein analysis of my blood shows the baby is healthy. Last year, Brandy and Monica came out with the song "The Boy is Mine." I keep playing this song on repeat because I don't have money for another tape. I keep it in my Walkman as I walk around

## MONTH THREE: FOOD DIARY

the condo, often stopping for breaks to breathe and remembering my life before I was *Pregnorant.*

- *Chamomile tea. I like the comfort and warmth of tea.*

Wake and weigh myself in the middle of the night; I am 122 pounds. I have never weighed so much in my life. Rumors that Henry was caught doing ecstasy flood my phone today. No one has any real details, just a different rendition of the same story. "He's doing drugs now. He's stealing. He got kicked out of school," they tell me over and over. I don't blink. I do not flinch.

I take a nap in the middle of the day and dream my baby will be stillborn.

- *Wake up and brew the hottest pot of tea I can stand.*

## MONTH THREE: FOOD DIARY

Sleep. Wake. Sleep. Waking while sleeptalking to myself:

"I love you," Henry says.

"I love you too," I say.

"I love you more, I love you more, more, more more, now hang up."

"I love you infinity plus a million, so you have to hang up," I tease back.

"No, you," he repeats.

"No… if you hang up I'll feel like… like… like I hung up on you," I stutter as we both laugh together.

## MONTH THREE: FOOD DIARY

"I won't hang up first so you won't have a choice…" I hear him tell me.

I am jarred awake in the middle of the night by these memories. In the dark, I grab a marker that happens to be red and permanent. I scribble on my sheet my favorite quote from Winston Churchill: "If you are going through hell, keep going." Dry heave.

## MONTH FOUR:

## GROUND

I cannot stop thinking maybe I should have just gotten the fucking abortion. *Maybe I should have just gotten the fucking abortion.* Maybe. I will not wake up in this tiny apartment; two windows in my bedroom one more morning without craving lemon cake, having an upset stomach, or remembering the look of the lady in the clinic, her eyes begging me, begging me not to delete my little... I will not not like the black-and-white swirled marble dresser, I will not not like the gray industrial carpet in this apartment because I like softer carpet, softer things, softer and personally picked with love like the carpet Mama and Daddy

## MONTH FOUR: GROUND

picked out when we lived together as a family in the old house. I will not like the hand-me-down condo that was my sister's—Mama has to live in it since my sister left to live in Virginia. I will not keep going to the bathroom fifteen gazillion times an hour with only a squelch of urine.

I will not regret I hand-picked him because he was a dancer. I will not forget he used to do what was then called the "crip walk" a dance based on a street gang. A dance that looked a lot like fancy footwork caused by an extreme nervous disorder, with Henry resembling a gyrating hyena on some type of upper.

I will not admit I wanted to get to know him. I will not remember my father—so naïve. Took myself and three of my closest "fake" friends to a teenage club once a week. He felt it was safe after we told him it was in the same building as a church. I will not recall if

## MONTH FOUR: GROUND

that were so, but it sounded nice enough and since the club was in the heart of one of the worst neighborhoods in Los Angeles, that meant the club was an incredibly interesting place to be. I will not think of the way my friends nicknamed it the "Soda Pop" club because saying something was "poppin'" was slang for saying this was somewhere I might find someone to make me feel better about myself.

I will not recall Henry at all. I will not remember his wisecracks, his slight bowlegged-ness I admired. I will not remember how he walked. I will not recall that everything he said was a joke. Maybe I should have just gotten the fucking abortion. I will not stare out this window at the squirrels. As I stare at the window, I remember the way Henry used to climb through the window at Daddy's.

## MONTH FOUR: GROUND

*I will not knock my forehead against the table until I recall until I remember until I can remember until I can surrender enough until I can remember this:*

Henry snuck in the window of my old dusty antique house. He was wearing a white shirt with a navy stripe along the bottom. I was supposed to be supervised. Dad never should've hired Martha as a maid, but I loved her because she ignored our cursing and let me and my best friends pull all the couch pillows off and scatter them across the living room and jump, even if we held plastic bowls of ice cream.

At first, Martha used to clean twice a week, but the counters were still dusty. One day, she must have felt superhuman and did better than usual. That day, Mama started to talk to her and found out she was homeless. Ma convinced Dad to let her live in and stay in the

## MONTH FOUR: GROUND

converted garage in the back of the new house we'd moved to. At least that's how I remembered it. Ma could've also picked her up clean off the side of the road—the damn girl was just *that* talkative.

Martha was a lanky RuPaul look-alike with one front tooth in the middle of her upper gums and a goblin laugh. She wore legging shorts with a white undershirt when she cleaned. Yes, you read that correctly, there's a good chance Ma brought a homeless person home, and she became our maid. Yes, Ma was just *that* kind… er, sort of.

I used to sucker my way into a ride home from any friend I could. I tried to cause Daddy less stress; his business wasn't doing so well, and he was never home. Latchkey was as empty as the new house

## MONTH FOUR: GROUND

was spooky, and Martha tried to look out, but usually she just let me do anything that might have made me smile.

I keep staring at the window, remembering the afternoon I'd helped Henry in by his jacket, dusting the bushes off. He clumsily dropped inside my room.

I knocked on the serving door on the wall; it connected my room to the kitchen. I would tease my dad about this feature in the house because it was like a lazy window meets a witch window. Everyone who saw it laughed at it until I told them what skinny coffin windows were said to be used for, and then they shut up.

I knocked and got Martha's attention. I asked her politely if she could make me a peanut butter and jelly sandwich in four diamond shapes. She said she would. When she was finished, she knocked

## MONTH FOUR: GROUND

softly. I slid the door upward, grabbed the sandwich, and closed it. Henry's big bold eyes peered at me, then the sandwich. I studied his long fingers, bounced my shoulders up and down, and fidgeted with the edge of his shirt, our faces so close I could smell the pores of his skin; the addictive smell of clean and cologne snuck up my nose.

I sat then rolled to a stand on my daybed and knocked on the serving door, pulled it up, and told her I was really, really hungry today and knew I was going to need another sandwich. Three minutes later, she knocked at the serving door.

I passed the other sandwich to Henry, and we giggled without sound as he looked at the slices. I was enamored with his charm, the creases around his lips, dimples over henna-hazel cheeks, the way his head was bizarrely shaped—elongated. Henry devoured the shapes as I was just finishing my second shape. I knocked

## MONTH FOUR: GROUND

softly on the serving door again. Martha answered as she swept the kitchen.

I told her I was really, really, *really* hungry and could use one more of those peanut butter and jelly sandwiches. A few moments went by and Martha knocked, shaking her head.

"All a dem there laloonies keep on eatin' up all the foods in the 'frigeratah!" she protested with her fist high in the air. Sandwiches kept appearing.

I hollered out in laughter as Henry hunched over, face to the carpet in another silent laugh, trying to keep from making any noise.

Henry and I held our breath to keep from bursting out. He ate all of the sandwich slices except one. I laughed until all of the muscles in

## MONTH FOUR: GROUND

my stomach were throbbing giddily. He ate everything, never offering me any.

I will not remember the phone ringing and snapping me from thoughts of Henry's selfishness. I will not remember the girl who called; her name was Tiffany, which I knew was a fake name. She asked questions about when the baby was conceived. And then she said something that made me stop breathing a bit:

"Henry says he wasn't with you, so you can't be pregnant with his baby," the loudmouth girl snapped at me. Her tone made rocks form in my throat.

"That can't be possible. Henry and I, we had… he took my virginity. I haven't been with anyone else, so—" I told her, voice shaking.

## MONTH FOUR: GROUND

I heard laughter on the line, like a few people were listening in.

"Well, he don't want you 'cuz he been with me the whole time," she interrupted.

Right then I wished I hadn't answered the phone. I found it funny how Henry couldn't call to check on me, but random girls named "Tiffany" could.

Breathe again.

I will not choose to.

I will not stop remembering the first time I met Henry's dad, Henry Sr., and he was jumbotron-tall to me. I will not erase his wife barking orders at him. I will not forget his nose spread across his face, much like his son's, and large hands and feet, a profuse

## MONTH FOUR: GROUND

stutter, and he drank beer in a green-necked bottle. I will not remember anything other than the way he bragged about his retirement being over half a million dollars from whatever loser-esque job I imagine he worked, maybe a Heineken factory. I will not recall he never spoke one word to me after I became pregnant—like I wasn't there.

I will not remember most of the people I know with big noses are liars, and maybe their noses grow an unnoticeable amount with every lie they tell, and soon, voilà, gargantuan schnozzes cover their faces. This is the reason both Henry and his father are liars. Or maybe it isn't their noses at all, just in their DNA. I will not stop thinking maybe I should have just gotten the fucking abortion.

I watch the squirrel out of the window. As it notices me, it scurries away with something in its cheek, stealing from the tree—so high

## MONTH FOUR: GROUND

up, so unafraid. I am reminded. I will not forget the time Henry and I went out for one of our one-month anniversaries.

Since he couldn't drive yet, his homeboy Ashley drove us in his beat-up jalopy. Others were to meet us there. It was the nicest restaurant I'd ever been to. Often my dad had taken my family to Gladstone's on Pacific Coast Highway, and we'd cracked open peanuts and watched frantic lobsters tap at their tanks, but never anything like this. We were at Houston's restaurant in Manhattan Beach, and I was dressed up fancily in my fake pearls and a dress that made me look at least two years older than I was, and I was tingling with glee. I wore red, and Henry kept telling me how much he didn't like that color. We arrived (without a reservation) at the restaurant, a dark wood den that looked as if the ceiling were too low. Dishes clanked and people laughed, the sound of bustling random couples enjoying themselves. The hostess

## MONTH FOUR: GROUND

seated our party, which had grown to at least five more strangers, possibly seven, but I will not remember I ate the shrimp tempura without knowing what tempura meant. The tempura arrived with a succulent sauce, and I grabbed a shrimp, which melted in my mouth. Henry sat next to me, occasionally reaching for my hand and squeezing it three times to say he loved me. No one introduced himself or herself, and I found it odd. No one else spoke up; I wasn't going to break the eating silence. They ordered. Boy, did they order. Hefty plates of food kept arriving. Everyone spoke simultaneously—making jokes and talking about the rest of the crew who wasn't there. I felt accepted, but strange. Toward the end of dinner, one by one, then two by one, people got up from the table for the bathroom, or some of them mumbled, "Smoke break." I didn't smoke, so I just nodded.

"You ready?" Henry looked at me, tilting his head toward the door.

## MONTH FOUR: GROUND

I thought to myself: *Ready for what?* We were the last two left at the table. I stared, perplexed. No one returned. Henry smirked, took off toward the door. I sat at the table, slowly folding a napkin as a souvenir in my purse. The waiter passed and dropped a padded folder in the middle of the table, and I reached in my pocket for my seven dollars. I opened the folder and realized I was alone at the table with an enormous bill. I kept asking myself: *Where is Henry?* I looked toward the window at the two people smoking. The one girl I'd just eaten with was walking hastily toward the parking lot. Panic shot through my arm. As I got up, I ran, tripped. I reached the bathroom, naively trying to balance in my heels. Washed my hands over and over. Checked the mirror. Fiddled with my purse strap. Hoped and hoped that Henry or one of the bourgeoisie girls I'd just shared a meal with but didn't know the names of would come to my rescue.

## MONTH FOUR: GROUND

If I called my dad, he would know I wasn't at Mari's like I'd said I was. If I called my mom, she would be incensed and disappointed and know Henry was involved. No one in this group was going to pay for two hundred and seventy three dollars' worth of food. When I cracked the bathroom door, the place still buzzed with people, the waiter bouncing around with no worries. My heart sank, jumped, then trembled in a rage I tried to keep subtle. I jumped up and down behind the bathroom door, preparing myself. I quickly skirted out of the bathroom, rounded the corner of the booth we'd sat in, opened our tab, threw my crumpled dollars in, and set off out the front door.

When I got outside, no one was there. Nothing but empty concrete as far as I could see. I started running across the lot without anything in sight. As tears came on, I spotted Ashley's jalopy with

## MONTH FOUR: GROUND

the blinkers on. In slow motion, I took off to the car, running like a loopy bird to the corner where the engine ran hot, smoky.

I did not speak a word on the ride home. I looked down at Henry's hand as he squeezed the back of my palm three times in a row, his eyes drilling into me. I could not feel anything.

I knew Henry wasn't like his friends. That this wasn't his idea. When Ashley drove the car into my mom's condominium, my eyes began to fill with water. I couldn't know if it was because of the way the night had gone or if it was because I needed to know this wasn't the kind of person he was. I was also upset the night was over and it'd be another week before we'd see each other. When I looked over at him, I knew he wanted to say something to me, but we were in the car, in front of Ashley. Instead, he just squeezed my

## MONTH FOUR: GROUND

hand tightly the whole ride home. I never got the chance to be as angry as I knew I was.

While this was all unfolding, Ma cracked the tip of her grapefruit juice open; next was gin. She prepared her nightly escape. I will not remember the way I felt in the car that night was the same way I feel today, four months Pregnorant, wishing he were more than just someone who ran out when it was time to pay.

I will not think about the possibility that if Henry and I had talked over my pregnancy face-to-face, things might have been different.

I will not feel the creases in my face after being in bed for nine hours, after I hear Ma leave and then return. I will not remember my memory flashing back about how ecstatic I was to be on the Blanco cheer squad, even when my left leg was seconds late,

## MONTH FOUR: GROUND

costing my team a perfect score. I will not remember the nice curvature of my waist or my tiny B cup, my wavy figure. I will not remember I could not see my waistline anymore or that I could pinch a Pillsbury dough roll from my stomach.

I will not think of my poetry, my poetry, and my poetry. I will not sit in a hunched-over sob. I will not find anything on television. I will not call my daddy, call my daddy only to receive his answering machine over and over. Maybe I should have just gotten the fucking abortion. Maybe.

I will not glance at my mother above my dinner plate listening to her warn me again: "This is yorrrrrr baby, not mine, so you will be raising this child, not me. No sirrrreee." I will not hold on to my stomach like my baby will fall out. I will not feel as if I have no worth or purpose except giving birth to this child.

## MONTH FOUR: GROUND

Instead of empowerment, I feel useless now. Like the many statistics I've seen on television. Like I don't know anything to teach my child, and there is no way I'll learn all I need to teach my baby before he or she is born. Helplessness sets in.

I will not forget Henry coming over a few days ago. (It will be the one and only time he comes to see me pregnant other than at my baby shower.) I will not stare at my growing belly. I will not tell Henry I love him I love him I love him, I love. I will not remain silent when he is at the door—my four-month pregnant belly bulging like six months. I will not hold the roundness in my hand like I usually do. I will not expect him to be used to it. I will not watch his eyes never look up once at mine but rather jump around, following my hands making circular motions around my roundness. I will not watch him stare horrified at my unfamiliar

## MONTH FOUR: GROUND

belly. I will not imagine he thinks I'm so fat. I will not remember him on the black leatherette couch staring at my belly, how I held it ever so delicately. I will not recall he never looked up, never once. It was *real* to him. I will not recall he never looked me in my eyes as he made his promises once again to visit often and go to my doctor's appointments. I will not remember his voice as he promised to be there for our baby while his eyes confirmed we would never be together again. I will not memorize the shake in his voice, the whimper in his stutter, the weakness he shrugged off nonchalantly. I will not recall the power having his child inside of me held or the paralysis having his baby inside of me gave. I was there again, at the table, Houston's restaurant, holding the bill. I will not recall having not only nothing to look to or live for, but not anything much to die for, except for maybe the moment when Henry looked back at his dead girlfriend and unborn child, he

## MONTH FOUR: GROUND

might feel sorry, just a little teeny bit sorry, just a wee bit sad, and the possibility he'd feel anything for me again would be enough.

After Henry left the other night, I sat on that black leatherette couch for hours staring out the window. Thinking about the new shoes he had on, his usual cologne used to be so addicting, his creased collar shirt. I looked down at my house clothes. After so much time staring out of that window, I thought to myself again what my mom used to say: "Piss or get up off the pot!" Do something about it or let it all go. So I raised up the top-floor window hard as I could, and with one leg up, other leg slung over, I thought to myself: Henry just left my house without looking me in my face, without saying the word "family," without any chance of ever wanting or loving me. Killing myself is easier than raising my child alone. *Killing myself is easier than him not wanting me.*

## MONTH FOUR: GROUND

Killing myself is easier in my mind. Killing myself is easier than knowing I gave my body treasure, my heart, my mind, my every drop of thought and energy just to be around him so I could feel the strongest thing I'd ever felt: his attention. I wanted him to let me wear his jacket again, to fall asleep holding me around my waist and kiss my temples when I startled. I wanted him to show one sign that wasn't impartial to the reality he could no longer control. Because I couldn't control it either, but I was doing the best I could. I wanted him to make a joke about me, show me I still meant something. But that night, I finally realized I didn't mean anything to him, and killing myself was easier than dying while I was still alive.

I will not remember the ledge. I will not I will not I will not see my mom at the door—face bruised with shock as I sat at the

## MONTH FOUR: GROUND

windowsill in my panties, a cut-off T-shirt, and an open robe, belly exposed. I will not remember that in my dreams I fly with no parachute. I will not recall the window screen being off and me out on the edge, legs dangling. I will not remember Ma whispering gently, tiptoe-y, "Honey, if you…"

I will not recall looking up, scared as a kitten in a palm tree. I will not remember the urge to jump and fly out of the window, the undercurrent urge—to get back my wings.

I don't remember Ma's face twitched as she screamed a blurry, "Noooooooooo!"

I don't remember the mess I felt.

I don't remember it.

## MONTH FOUR: GROUND

Don't remember the cold metal ledge where the screen to the window should have been. Don't remember how dirty it was. Don't remember if it was cold or not. Don't remember my legs dangling on that edge hours after Henry left. Don't remember, but I knew he was never coming back the way he was before. Don't recall if he'd ever again be the sport junkie who used to whisper right into my lips that he loved me and he'd never leave me as long as we both shall live. Don't remember if he'd ever again be the person who promised me no matter what happened between us, we'd always be friends. Don't recall, but I was sure he was never coming back the same him again. Don't remember the horrible tears sick in my eyes the deep deep breath before jumping.

"You won't die! You won't die, you'll just be paralyzed!" Mama screamed out her lungs. "We're only on the second floor, you

## MONTH FOUR: GROUND

won't die, you'll be in a fucking wheelchair for the rest of your fucking life and you'll lose your baby, which seems to be the only fucking thing you care about these days! So go'n 'head if you want to be stupid!"

Don't remember climbing my heavier-than-usual self back inside. Don't remember why in the world I didn't jump.

I do remember that Ma knew me well enough to know the more she pleaded with me not to jump, the more likely I would be to try my luck at flying. I do remember her holding me, rocking me hard hard hard back and forth on the black leatherette couch after she'd pulled me from the ledge onto the floor, and I do remember how unnaturally large her teardrops were as they seeped into her skin. I remember how I shook heavily and how she wrapped a fluffy lion blanket around me like I was a newborn. Remember how my belly

## MONTH FOUR: GROUND

protruded and how much I hated to look at myself like this. Remember thinking maybe I should have gotten the fucking abortion. Maybe I should have gotten the fucking abortion. Maybe.

"He doesn't love me he doesn't love me, he never did, he never will, he won't love the baby or me he—he—" I shivered, I rocked back and forth shaking my head harder the harder I rocked.

"He won't, baby, he won't. *You* have to love *you.* You have to love you, and I love you." Mama's bottom lip quivered then twitched.

I remember Ma had the screens put on all of the windows the next day. I remember I slept in that fluffy lion blanket she'd bought off the corner of Slauson Avenue. I slept in it every night thereafter. I remember Henry went to jail the next week for something petty

## MONTH FOUR: GROUND

and random that I can't remember. So many people I hardly knew kept calling to notify me. It was all a blur.

I remember Mama gave me life, and I remember she gave it to me twice when she kept me from jumping that night.

I remember feeling faint gas bubbles, once, then twice. Then a rolling feeling. I remember ignoring the feeling, and then I remember the twirling tickle again with more pressure. My baby was moving. *My baby was moving.*

I remember falling into the deepest sleep, as if my mind had actually jumped and my body needed to recover from realizing it hadn't.

# MONTH FIVE:

# DOPPELGÄNGER

**Doppelgänger** - *[DOP-uhl-gang-uhr] noun; 1. A ghostly double or counterpart of a living person. 2. Alter ego; double.*

I walked through school as my doppelgänger, dwindling away. Time had no start or stop as I attempted to make sense of my body by detaching from it. My small joys were putting eclectic words together, descriptions of people into neat piles. Making up their perspectives. Mocking people. Writing them as characters, defining family and friends. Experiences were a game of comfort. Involuntary crying went away. Patience went away with it. I

## MONTH FIVE: DOPPELGÄNGER

noticed behaviors for which I'd find an ideal word. Placed people in neat little cartons in my mind.

The days overlapped, entering different dimensions. Other than my belly—looking as if I'd overdosed on explosives—things didn't change or progress. People saw me and stalled. I was a bursting melon, a buttercup balloon. I was a walking full moon. People saw my belly before my face—my nose melting across my cheeks, stuck permanently blowing bubbles. *Well over* the time for me to transfer schools. Culver Park Continuation. School for slow-developing teens, for kids who misbehaved more than regular school could tolerate. Pregnant teens. Henry didn't have to change schools. I wasn't "bad" or "salacious." I was broken and hopeless. I missed many lessons. Threw up. Told myself I couldn't go. I learned morning sickness wasn't *always* just three months.

## MONTH FIVE: DOPPELGÄNGER

Tired. All day. Tired after sleeping pretty in a pink silk robe. Wake in wet sweat. Sleep hot. Breathless. I'm in a new school. Yes, Culver Park, where I'm introduced to a handful of other pregnant teenagers. Introduced to a writing teacher, Tatiana. She's jumpy but inspiring—better than paprika-salt-sugar. Animated and zesty, Tati's skin bloomed. Brown hair, barely looked twenty-one. Funny. Real, not robotic. She used her own experiences and examples in lessons. She cursed. I took her poetry class, hardly ever left. Mornings, I hung in her class doorway. Her brashness, the way she spoke in words like riddles—it kept her whole class intrigued. She wasn't afraid to use words I didn't know.

She required me to read Sandra Cisneros's *The House on Mango Street:* "Everything is holding its breath inside me."

## MONTH FIVE: DOPPELGÄNGER

Tati then demanded with a stern yet playful holler that I read Octavia Butler's *Kindred:* "I don't have a name for the thing that happened to me, but I don't feel safe anymore." I was overjoyed to have her as a teacher; she filled me full of knowledge. I began to read more than I ever had. If there was something I wanted to know, she didn't give me the answer but said, "Chica, go look it up!" Her voice was playfully commanding. The way every teacher should teach.

Days stopped irking me. I rushed my other work because I couldn't go to her class if I didn't finish the others. Didn't read the books she assigned initially, just wanted to write write write. Started interesting discussions about books I *said* I'd read. I nodded in class until I got enough of her calling on me when I wasn't sure.

## MONTH FIVE: DOPPELGÄNGER

She didn't treat me like I didn't know, even though I didn't. She didn't treat me "Pregnorant." She treated me like I was intelligent. I wanted to prove to her I was. I read everything I could, and I read it until I understood it enough to teach another person. I taught other people in my head—imitating her voice because it demanded attention. Her teaching method gave her control. I wanted control over myself, over information I retained, my life. Tati gave me triple doses with encouragement, creative words, and counseling. If I was wrong, she told me I was wrong in such a sarcastic but serious way it didn't hurt my feelings. I learned quickly how to recover from getting an answer wrong, and it became a game for me to challenge myself to know the right answers.

I found myself reading entire books late in the night, cover to cover. Began using big words around her like *ubiquitous* and

## MONTH FIVE: DOPPELGÄNGER

*temperance.* When I got to school, I was beaming. I was excited to discuss books with her. The more I came to her, the more she gave me. We talked about everything. She became my mentor, my teacher, my friend, and my sister. All in one.

I became me.

We began with a lesson in acrostic poetry—another way I'd found to compartmentalize my feelings. We'd pick a name or object and then as a class we'd describe it or bring it alive with poetry. This was when I noticed my hands were puffy and looked stubby. I wrote. At break, I inhaled a bag of Cheetos, shoveled sherbet ice cream down my hole, and followed it with a quesadilla, hold the sour cream. My body grew as fast as my mind, and I read. Between my memories and my lessons, I'd entered another dimension.

## MONTH FIVE: DOPPELGÄNGER

*P*anicked, perturbed, pained

*R*estless, resentful, rampage

*E*xasperated, expectant, embarrassed

*G*ullible, guilty, growing

*N*aïve, noisome, naked

*A*ngry, anxious, animated

*N*aughty, natural, nervous

*T*ense, tenacious, terrified

I laughed as I penned my first acrostic poem. I was able to sit back and look at myself for what I was: pregnant. I'd lost my true sense

## MONTH FIVE: DOPPELGÄNGER

of self. Everything I did revolved around my baby, but where was *I*? My will was gone because I'd thrown it away as punishment for the decision I made to give life to my child.

My body was sleepy, but my mind wanted to read nonstop. Sleep was inconvenient. I feared not having enough time to love myself and my child. I was afraid I wouldn't get my dreams or I'd have to choose between my dreams and my baby, and I wasn't happy about it but had no choice. Every day I had a new lesson, and every day it was the last class and the only class I looked forward to. That, and the hour for lunch.

I dreamed of being the poet laureate, another Rita Dove or a girl Robert Pinsky. I fell asleep to those visions. I woke falling off the side of the stage like a hippo-too-heavy. An obese disgrace of swollen cheeks and fists. Blimps don't get book tours.

## MONTH FIVE: DOPPELGÄNGER

I'd always been petite, four foot eleven. As a child, my godmom nicknamed me "Twiggi," as a twig branch, because I was teensy, three premature pounds at birth. There was a model named Twiggy as well, but I was never model-esque because I didn't have the height. I was a quiet child and kept to myself. This was often misread as stuck-up. I was caramel in the summer, and I had peachy cheeks over beige-brown skin in the winter. My hair was curly and knotted when wet, although I preferred it straight. I loved cotton candy, so the body sprays I wore made me smell of rose ice cream and vanilla cake. I never tired of that smell, but other smells were a different story: when Mama made cabbage, Cornish hens, or asparagus with turkey neck, I would choke in my chest, nauseous. I was shaped like an hourglass, and I only wore at least three-inch heels from the moment I tried my first pair on in Ross Dress for Less with Ma. I was around thirteen then. But today,

## MONTH FIVE: DOPPELGÄNGER

because my stomach was growing outward, I began to wear flats. I dared not attempt anything less comfortable. I could hardly stand as it was.

\*\*\*\*\*\*\*\*\*\*\*\*\*\*\*\*\*\*\*\*\*\*\*\*\*\*\*\*\*\*\*\*\*\*\*\*\*\*\*\*\*\*\*\*\*\*\*\*\*\*\*\*\*\*

The summer I was fifteen, my cousin Michael (who was seventeen then) lived with us for a while. Michael was the son of another of Ma's closest friends, Marianne. He was short, pretzel-colored, with a big thick shaved head and fat lips. He used to torture me by twisting a scarf tightly into a rat's tail and snapping it at my thighs. I ran screaming around the house, reddened thighs pulsating. Throughout those months, I learned a valuable lesson about my writing. One day, Michael read my personal diary aloud to everyone at the teen center. I'd hidden it under my pink pillow and had absolutely no idea when he'd retrieved it, but he'd held it over

## MONTH FIVE: DOPPELGÄNGER

my head knowing I was half his size and I'd never reach it. I'd lied and made up boyfriends when talking to my friends, telling them of people I'd kissed before, people who never existed. But details of my first *real* kiss slithered out of his mouth. My heart bled through my chest. I was angry at myself for having ever written anything down. From that point forward, I was sure, poetry was all I'd ever write. No documentation of anything. Just fantasy, *maybe*. Poetry. Yea, poetry.

> Disavowed - *[dis·a·vowed] verb; 1. To disclaim knowledge of, responsibility for, or association with. 2. To say firmly that you have no connection with someone or something; deny.*

I went from being Daddy's little girl to being a little whore, or so I felt. Daddy <u>disavowed</u> me after I became pregnant. I defined him

## MONTH FIVE: DOPPELGÄNGER

with the word disavowed because I liked how "smart" of a word it seemed to be. I made Daddy a character in my mind but put him in a trashcan pile. I said when I was stronger I'd unpack how he chose not to speak to me after I became pregnant. The last thing I'd wanted was to be pregnant. I'd only tried to be the best daughter I could be, which went as far as ninth grade. After ninth grade, I'd ruined my life as far as Dad was concerned, which he confirmed when he'd answer my phone calls and then hang up on me as though I were a telemarketer. How did I go from being the babygirl who Daddy used to bring overstuffed Christmas stockings, bikes, and computer games, to a person he couldn't call or name?

The first time I suspected something was wrong, Mama had taken me to the doctor because I was complaining of constipation after

## MONTH FIVE: DOPPELGÄNGER

Fletcher's Castoria, prune juice, and an enema hadn't worked. I marched in to the nurse, who hastily explained: "The bathroom is just down the hall, and if you could take this cup with you, I'll need a sterile urine sample."

"Mmm, k," I groaned. The office sent me home with instructions to drink a lot of water and wait for a bowel movement. Severe constipation prevailed.

Four or so business days later, I was propped up at Daddy's kitchen table using baby talk to try and get him to take me shopping. The table was covered in newspapers, coffee stains, a space heater, and a dusty radio with missing knobs and a foiled antenna. Mama had moved out almost three years prior; in her place, dust moved in. The phone rang, and as usual we couldn't find it. Daddy mumbled things about the cordless phone and the

## MONTH FIVE: DOPPELGÄNGER

way it behaved. At the last ring, Daddy picked up the phone. I could hear the answering machine coming on and a professional woman's voice talking in the background. She attempted to leave her message when I heard Daddy interrupt. "Oh, no, she's here, let me get her for you," he mumbled as he flung the phone out toward me, concern between his brows.

"Lalanii, this is Brenda from Dr. Kavin's office."

Her voice made my heartbeat stumble.

"Are you alone? I must discuss confidential information with you."

"Yeah, why, what's up?"

"Lalanii, your results came back from when you were in our office last week, and I must inform you that you are pregnant."

## MONTH FIVE: DOPPELGÄNGER

She'd just paralyzed me from the neck down. I became a wax figure. The cordless phone slipped from my hand onto the tile floor and burst into slow-motion pieces like a silent movie. I ran out of the kitchen in a panic as Daddy followed close behind. My heartbeat sank into my ears, racing even though time tiptoed in my head. All I kept saying was, "I am soOo fucked now, I am sOOOo fucked now." And I was.

"Now, what thhhh— what the hell is going on?" Daddy's voice was high-pitched.

Low moaning gulps, cries, shock-gasping, my head in my hands rocking back and forth, wailing. Wailing. Went down to a whimper, then went up again, wailing.

## MONTH FIVE: DOPPELGÄNGER

**Flagrant** - *[fley·gruh·nt] adjective; 1. Shockingly noticeable or evident; obvious; glaring: a flagrant error. 2. Notorious; scandalous: a flagrant crime; a flagrant offender. 3. Archaic, blazing, burning, or glowing.*

I never bothered to know my sister, Serena. Growing up, she was boisterous and flagrant, and I put her in a box marked "fifteen years older than I." She spoke in a turned-up voice, almost like she was hard of hearing, which might have been true. We grew up in the same house, but her dad died—so Daddy took her in as his. It never occurred to me that she was my stepsister; she was just my sister. A true sister with all that hatelove. My ears blurred with the noise of her.

My sister's boyfriend got her pregnant, and she returned from somewhere off Wilshire, or was it Vegas–married and glowing,

## MONTH FIVE: DOPPELGÄNGER

like Lauryn Hill in her heyday. Mama and Daddy moved Serena out of the bedroom upstairs next to mine into the two-bedroom apartment behind us on our property. Daddy wasn't happy but did the best he could and gave her new husband, Warren, a job at his graphics company. Warren was an Ice Cube look-alike with a bad smoking habit. He was talented but a jerk, cocky, clever, and sneaky.

Warren paid rent to Daddy every so often, and Ma switched out telephone and electric bills so Daddy wouldn't know he was paying for both households. Eight or so years later, I remember Serena's annoying daughter Oleana stealing my lip glosses and clear mascara; my nephew Dane, a few years younger, was what I liked to call "snaggletoof." And her latest addition in the last few months—Valerie—did nothing but cry and ieeeeeehkk.

## MONTH FIVE: DOPPELGÄNGER

Yes, after one baby came another, then a third, and my sister started screeching instead of talking, and she became extremely nosy. This translated into her being the most bothersome person in the universe.

After getting the news I was pregnant, I dashed to the other cordless handset and ran to the backyard as far as I could go. I called my sister, who'd by then moved to Virginia, because life there was cheaper. Serena was home. "Hey, Twiggi, whatchoo doooooin?"

"Ree-ree ..." My voice cracked. Birds went silent, the wind blew away.

"Whassamatter, Twiggi? What's wrong?" her voice rose. Cue up full tears and theatrics. The cry came out from my gut as I dug my nails in the powdered dirt in the backyard behind the unkept

## MONTH FIVE: DOPPELGÄNGER

garden. I broke into a fever sweat. "Oh, Twiggi, you're pregnant!" She guessed the truth in a high-pitched scream.

I don't know if she guessed because I was at that age where teenagers lose their virginity, or because I used to be unusually prissy and nerdy in her presence, or because she'd known of my boyfriend. But I do know that without saying much else, we'd come to an understanding. That day, as I sat with my legs crossed beneath the tomato vines, next to the avocado tree that wasn't growing. I sat there for hours as she coached me through what I should say to Daddy. I listened as she told me he was still going to love me and he wouldn't think bad things about me.

"But, Ree-Ree, it was one time! It was only one time!! I love him. I love him so much I'd die for him." Technically, it was more than one time, but who was actually counting at a time like this?

## MONTH FIVE: DOPPELGÄNGER

The idea that I'd let Henry inside of me without being willing to die for him wasn't ok with me because I knew the consequences of having sex. I loved it when he tickled me, I loved it when we made references to things out loud at the same time, I loved it when he held my hand and pulled my arm close into him to kiss my face. I hated being without him so much I wanted to die if he didn't want me.

Serena listened as I told her about Henry. She was treating me like a baby. She spoke to me about a big decision I had to make. She asked me about Henry's whereabouts. She asked how I was doing in school. She told me I needed to go tell Daddy and go over to Mama's house so I could tell her as well. I shook my head, and she responded as though she could see.

"I can't tell anyone I can't tell them what I've done! I can't I just can't I can't tell them I've messed up my entire life."

## MONTH FIVE: DOPPELGÄNGER

My sister gave advice with more love than I ever knew she had for me, and she told me about some of her own imperfections, confessing that when she married Warren, none of the family was on her side. This was reassuring. I slumped my shoulders and smiled. When I hung up the phone, Dad came out from behind the garage. He had been listening, and his glasses were foggy, cheeks flushed pink like raw hot steam had burned them.

•

> Foulmouthed - *[foul-mouth d, -moutht] adjective; 1. Using obscene, profane, or scurrilous language; given to filthy or abusive speech.*

I overheard an argument between two raunchy misfits in the building across from me and worried about how things would be at

## MONTH FIVE: DOPPELGÄNGER

this school. The arguing jarred a memory of when Mama and Daddy were still together and we lived in the old brick house in Culver City with the non-paying tenant Beatrice in the backhouse at the bottom and my sister (who was knocked-up at that time) in the two-bedroom above.

Mama was <u>foulmouthed</u> and used to scream a lot. I remembered I was around ten when she chased me with an envelope, waving it in her hand back and forth. She ran the up the stairs cursing. I'd used my brand-new white socks to tie around the front of my knees.

"I know you must be out of your damn mind, crazy-ass child!" she hollered as she ran after me. I'd invited my best friend Kaitlynn to pretend we were puppies—barking at each other across the front yard. Kaitlynn was the neighbor across the street, a pale girl with long brown hair and eyes that changed color. I'd gone out on the

## MONTH FIVE: DOPPELGÄNGER

front lawn filled with merriment, and in the heat of the moment Kaitlynn and I were growling on all fours as we stained all of my socks with grass and mud. Kaitlynn ran back home across the street without looking, like a punished pup. She'd heard Ma's yells.

Ma reached the top of the stairs and turned the corner into my princess room. As she charged toward me, I panicked and grabbed the window and flung it back as hard as I could. I put one leg out on the ledge, then the other, and as she cursed at me, I jumped. I landed lightly on the top of the roof. Mama saw I was safe and urged me to come inside. The more she pressured, the farther out onto the roof I went. Farther and farther, until finally she realized the only way to get me to come back was to leave me to myself. From that point on, any time I got into trouble—any time I needed

## MONTH FIVE: DOPPELGÄNGER

to think, read, breathe, or be—off to the roof I went. This prevented her from attempting to murder me. It became so common she would just open the kitchen window downstairs and scream to me upstairs on the roof when it was time to eat.

All I knew how to do was run.

> **Imaginative** - *[ih-maj-uh-nuh-tiv, -ney-tiv] adjective; 1. Creative, inventive, clever, ingenious. 2. Having exceptional powers of imagination. Lacking truth; fanciful.*

I was probably around eleven when my imaginative side took over. Sometimes I would sneak down my stairs and see Daddy with his

## MONTH FIVE: DOPPELGÄNGER

glasses on, his eyebrows scrunched together as he waited at the kitchen table that smelled of strong black coffee. He learned to drink it black because he said some places he'd go wouldn't have what he needed, so he had to acquire a taste for it in its natural state. I'd peek at him, and as soon as I saw him reading the newspaper, it gave me nervous energy. I would run back upstairs, open the window in my room, and slowly climb onto the top of the roof and do just as he was doing, sit and read. Sit, write. Afternoons, there was shade, and dreams became real. For hours, no one would miss me, and I would sit on the roof wishing I had wings to catch a breeze and be back before dinner. I learned to love reading, thinking, and being alone because, just as Dad said: "I'd have to make do with what I had." Some places I'd go wouldn't have the friendships I'd need. I'd have to acquire a zeal for life through reading and documenting experiences.

## MONTH FIVE: DOPPELGÄNGER

I'd planned to become a lawyer, but that would've been only to appease my Daddy. What really excited me was rushing into bookstores like they were toy stores and coming out with a shameless smile and cheap romance—maybe some risqué poetry. The home I grew up in was a two-story house with a sky-blue view from my window of a big tree with humongous roots. Daddy told me he was born in a small place called Turtle Bay on the north shore of Oahu. Hawaii. Turtle Bay was known mostly as a vacation spot, yet Daddy was nothing but a well-preserved workaholic. He met Ma when he moved to Los Angeles after being in the service, although I never knew much of his past. Everything he said could have been made up because he read so much. All I really knew of Daddy was he owned a Porsche at a time when most people didn't own nice cars because they were too expensive. As his graphics and design business took off, I saw less and less of

## MONTH FIVE: DOPPELGÄNGER

him, as did Mama. He was in love with his art the way I was in love with words. There is something to be said about a person who disappears. But there is more to be said about a person who disappears at the times when you need them the most, especially when you live in the same household. "Work was Daddy's mistress," Ma had said under her breath once, but I didn't know if I'd heard her right—perhaps she'd said she was "just stressed."

When I finally looked up, Tati was smacking me in the back of the head with a literary magazine. I didn't even remember how I'd made it into the classroom, but she was encouraging us to now elaborate more on our assignment. I quickly wrote an acrostic poem about my Daddy. Once I'd learned the technique well enough, I began to bend the rules. This was when Tati introduced

## MONTH FIVE: DOPPELGÄNGER

me to what I'd done naturally with partial rhyme and alliteration. She egged me on, pushing me to go where my words went.

Frantic. Fragile. Future.

Abortion. Absence. Absolution.

Truant. Totality. Thank you.

Hindsight. Humiliated. Hero.

Ebullient. Ethereal. Enraged.

Resolute. Relinquish. Reverse.

Again I searched for more definitions, more words, and more ideas I could use to articulate. I had to go to a fat girls/no hope school because getting my diploma might give me a chance in the real world, a world my now-Pregnorant statistics didn't stand a chance

## MONTH FIVE: DOPPELGÄNGER

in anyway. One moment, I was excited about the promise of learning and furthering my education; the next morning, I was thinking of scapegoats if being a mother got too hard for me. I just couldn't get over that I was forced to go to a blubber ball/overdumb school because I was the dummy with a tummy who trusted somebody, who trusted some dummy. Adrenaline began to pump adrenaline equal to the pace of my thoughts. For Henry, I wrote a haiku:

Oblivious

Almost family

Can't remember your best friend.

No more reminders.

## MONTH FIVE: DOPPELGÄNGER

Then I wrote an acrostic for him. Tried to do homework; instead, acrostic poems came out.

**C**areless, cow, crock

**O**btuse, oblique, overwhelmed

**W**ayward, wicked, wimp

**A**fraid, arrogant, animalistic

**R**eckless, radical, rancorous

**D**eceiving, devoid, devious

## MONTH FIVE: DOPPELGÄNGER

The next time I looked up, I was home with my journals splayed across my twin bed. I was lost in Tati's assignments and the thoughts they provoked within. The school wasn't so bad. By the time I was almost finished, I realized my body was slightly cramping, my right leg shaking—which was the moment I realized I'd been grabbing my stomach tightly for some time. I was almost five months pregnant. My head felt light and my palms were sweating. My whole body was uncomfortable. I felt strange, like I needed to use the bathroom, but my heart quickened. My teeth shivered. My eyes were swelling up with water, but I wasn't crying. I rushed to the bathroom, staring at the wannabee marble floor. I must've lost track of time because it was dark out. I tried to urinate. Nothing but a few drops came out. I wiped gingerly with the tissue and as I went to throw it in the toilet, I saw thick streaks of blood. I held my breath until I couldn't anymore. A guttural

## MONTH FIVE: DOPPELGÄNGER

scream as I raced to the phone to dial Mama—my hand shaking profusely. I misdialed twice, then a busy signal. I dialed again. Busy again.

# MONTH SIX:

# SLEEPTALKING NAKED

*Dear diary,*

*We were naked. I kept my socks on. Maybe I should go backward—we weren't naked yet. We were walking. Last night, Henry and I went walking around the complex Ma moved to after the split. We were holding hands, so full of touching. We walked around, and Henry pinned me up against garage 182 for a kiss and my heart grew glitter.*

## MONTH SIX: SLEEPTALKING NAKED

I pulled the tissue of blood closer to my face as I held my stomach, wincing. I threw the blood-soaked tissue and grabbed hold of the marble-top sink to keep myself up. My other hand went to autopilot redial, and I remembered the day Henry and I walked around Cameo Woods. I hated Cameo Woods. It was a private community on the outskirts of Culver City. I would go there on the weekends, after my parents broke into pieces, because Ma lived there now, after my sis moved her family to the east coast. Henry and I walked around the walkway of the condominium toward the tennis court. I remembered he took his racket and hit as many tennis balls at me (back to back) as he could, while I yelped and ran from them. That was the fun. Me running, him hitting them at me. Horseplay and absurdity as usual. As I walked, he took one foot and put it in front of me to trip me, I would catch myself and notice his hands out to catch me in case I didn't (catch myself). I would hit

## MONTH SIX: SLEEPTALKING NAKED

him, then hug him, and again with the kissing. This night, we walked around the condo forever in circles. We dillydallied around the dirty patches of grass (mingling with green). I picked beige dandelions and as I blew them, he pretended to squeeze them.

"Would you love me if I had no hair?"

"I would love you if you had no hair, half a leg, one front tooth, and hobbled after me like this." He imitated hopping along, a goofy look on his face. I laughed and pushed him as hard as I could. He pretended to fall over harder than I'd pushed. We meandered around until we found the laundry room. Someone was drying their clothes; the smell was warm air and Downy dryer sheets. The person had left the door cracked, intending to come back without needing a key. We snuck in. I climbed first atop the

## MONTH SIX: SLEEPTALKING NAKED

folding table and walked across to the two dryers. I sat atop the dryer near the window. Henry cut the light.

We'd talked about making love for at least three months. I was curious, and a friend of mine, Nia, told me how it felt. She had large breasts and a top-heavy hourglass figure, and everyone knew she was having lots of sex. She talked about sex in detail. Henry and I had been dating for over a year. I'd told him repeatedly he would have to date me that long before I would consider being intimate. Nia said after I had sex, I would like it so much I would want to have sex all of the time. I was afraid, but my fear wasn't strong enough around Henry. I wanted him with serious curiosity, in the way I wanted to ditch school but didn't have the courage.

## MONTH SIX: SLEEPTALKING NAKED

Henry kissed me slowly in the laundry room. He wasn't urgent or restless like before we started kissing a lot. He knew how to follow and taught me how to follow. He was my first kiss, but that was *my* secret, that first kiss was a secret I'd keep. I told him everything else, except that he truly was my first real kiss.

I told him about the alligator my Dad had in our backyard when I was little. That the alligator lived inside my Dad's compost machine and ate all of the decomposing food we fed him. Later, I told him I'd seen the alligator and he should come to see it too. He laughed from his stomach as his eyes got larger, teasing me. A few days later, he asked about the alligator, and I was sad to tell him it had only been a lizard. He laughed harder, holding his stomach, mumbling something about me and my imagination.

## MONTH SIX: SLEEPTALKING NAKED

Henry had his hands down my gray sweats now. Oh shit. His hands were touching my soft patch of hair. Mingling between me. Oh shit. The tiny window of the laundry room fogged. His hands were soft and languid. He was unafraid. I remember when we'd meet up after school; he'd always hold my hand. I'd look down at his hands, and his nails were always clean. His pants were freshly ironed and smelled of starch and, again, clean. Being this close to him made me flex my pelvic muscles and squeeze them together tightly. His hands were bracing my back, and our breathing matched. We had been kissing so long it felt chapped and tight above my lips.

We had a relationship over the phone since we were in the tenth grade and neither one of us could drive. Sometimes we'd see each other if we could arrange to meet at certain places.

## MONTH SIX: SLEEPTALKING NAKED

My thoughts flashed to him one night in his uniform. We were at a football game, and he wore a royal blue bowtie. When I saw him, everything around him was in black and white and the bowtie was bright blue. His face was vibrant. After we'd known each other a week, we were inseparable.

I'd call, he'd call. We'd stay on the phone so long we'd fall asleep; I'd wake up to the dial tone lady *eek*ing in my ear. This was what I liked to call sleeptalking. I'd say something completely incomprehensible, something incoherent, and I'd pretend I wasn't sleepy in order to keep him on the phone longer.

Most times we'd start our conversation at nine thirty at night and stay on the phone until ten in the morning. All would be quiet, and then suddenly his squeaking mother would pick up the phone and say, "Henry! I need the phone right now, you've been on this

## MONTH SIX: SLEEPTALKING NAKED

phone all damn night!" I chuckled, and we said our I love yous, over, and over, and over. Twenty minutes later, he called me back and I answered the phone, "I love you," since I saw his number on the caller ID. He'd hear me and repeat it, and I heard his mother in the background screaming at him about chores. I heard him holler back, "Shut the fuck up, muuh-fuckah." I paid it no attention. It was really annoying to be interrupted when you're on the phone. I remembered this as I felt my chapped lips.

Henry and I left the laundry room, and I was googly knowing I'd gone further than usual, further than I'd wanted to. We talked about a rumor of his friend and a girl I knew. They were smitten with each other, but not the way we were. We put them to a *tsk tsk tsk*—shame. I jumped on his back as we left. He started to twirl me

## MONTH SIX: SLEEPTALKING NAKED

around. I started to squeeze him around the neck. We saw it was getting dark. We'd been gone for hours.

"Where's your mom think you are?"

"At Ashley's." He spoke of his homeboy nonchalantly.

"What time is he coming to get you?"

"When I call him." Henry shrugged. "Where's your mom think you are?"

"In my room." We both snickered. We walked along the pathway, and I looked up at the stars. They were blinking. I can't remember if there was a moon. "I've never felt like this about anyone, Henry," I said.

## MONTH SIX: SLEEPTALKING NAKED

Henry handed me a note he'd written. I'd been asking him to write me a poem about his feelings for me for over a year. He'd explained he didn't like to write because every time he did, it hurt. I chuckled and told him if he loved me he would write me a letter—at least. That night, I read that letter. It was scribbled, or written as though it was tagged, with bold overlapping letters in passionate red ink:

MONTH SIX: SLEEPTALKING NAKED

Lalanii,

I am finally writing you. This really isn't that bad. I just wanted to let you know that I love you very much and you make me happy. When I am around you I laugh and smile. You are the prettiest girl in the world. One day we will get married and live happily ever after. I cannot even believe you are my girlfriend. You are very special to me. I love you.

Love,

Henry

## MONTH SIX: SLEEPTALKING NAKED

He stood to the side watching me read it, leaning against the wall. When I finished, I ran over and kissed him, throwing my hands out happily, letter in hand as he smiled. His eyes were so brown (under the night's light) against the orange streetlight's glare.

We walked down a pathway behind someone's place. Behind the trash bins, behind another laundry facility with two washers going and going. We held hands as we walked to the corner of one of the condos inside the complex; it seemed to have a backyard. I could hear the cars on the street. I ran over as I noticed a play set I'd never seen before. It had a wavy slide attached to the side, and it was chipped and yellow. There were old tires attached on one side where children could climb up. There was a ladder, and there was a very tiny slide covered in dirt. I ran on top of it and then climbed down the side. I slipped under the bottom. Henry

## MONTH SIX: SLEEPTALKING NAKED

followed, imitating Tarzan by hanging on the set, then he slid under. Kissed me.

Kept kissing me, this time stronger.

"You love me, right?"

"Of course I love you." He kissed me. I kissed his neck. He kissed mine.

Henry took off his jacket and laid it on the grass so I wouldn't mess up my sweatpants. The grass was damp. It was crisp outside, early spring, my favorite time of year. I could see, faded in the background, a garden of sorts with grass that grew up the walls. His breath smelled like I wanted to swallow it. I grabbed the pole of the play set to brace myself, and my palms were wet with dew.

## MONTH SIX: SLEEPTALKING NAKED

He touched my back and undid my bra. I slowly slipped backward on the yellowing grass. He lifted my shirt; my nipples were shrinking to shriveled points. I looked at them in awe and watched him fondle them in his mouth. He slipped his jeans belt off and slid down his zipper. My heart—quicksand. I rubbed along his chest. I smelled his neck. I breathed him in like the permanent marker Ma always told me not to smell. I took another, deeper, higher. He pulled at my sweats, and I picked up my weight for him to slide them down farther. I wished I'd worn my prettier panties instead of these with the childish colorful hearts. He slid my shirt off. I shivered. He covered me with his sweater and I stayed lying down. He lifted the sweater to caress my breasts, and then I saw him fiddling. I assumed he was fiddling with a condom. Fear pumped through me, but I could not move. Oh shit. I Oh shit shit shit to myself. He leaned in—close to me—and I could sense him, then

## MONTH SIX: SLEEPTALKING NAKED

without warning I felt him move into where my body opened as he whispered,

"I love you, I love you, I love you, I won't hurt you. I love you."

I gasped and squeezed my eyes tightly. A tear came out. It felt as though something was ripping my skin, then stinging, but my body was too excited to say stop. He kissed my tear before it slid all the way down my face.

"You ok?"

"Mmm-hmm." I shook my head quickly.

He pushed in farther, and I cried out. He stopped held me and then moved slower inside of me. "You ok?"

## MONTH SIX: SLEEPTALKING NAKED

I shook my head no.

*Dear diary,*

*I shouldn't have done it but I wanted to feel closer to him. Henry holding me while he was inside me last night made me feel so protected. It was painful but I still don't really care because I wanted it. He kept his lips to mine tightly and that made me feel better. He smelled so good, even when he broke a sweat on the back of his neck. His dick was thick and long and I liked to look at it, just like Nia said I would. The whole time we were doing it I watched his stomach move as he went inside of me. He kept his eyes staring at me, telling me it was ok. He kept repeating himself. He kept asking me if I was ok. It didn't feel all that feel good, but I do feel older—like I've got a secret. I*

# MONTH SIX: SLEEPTALKING NAKED

*love him so much when I'm not around him, it hurts me. Between my legs I feel achy. I think we were doing it for a long time. Maybe I did ok. Sometimes I wanted him to stop but his facial expressions told me it felt good to him. I didn't want him to think it wasn't ok for me because then he probably wouldn't want me anymore. I could smell the way his scalp smelled, it made me excited. His hair was cut low and wavy and I think maybe he got a fresh haircut just to see me. Having sex was not what I thought it would be. I thought it would be sensual and my whole body would twinkle. Instead it felt like his dick was too big for my body. He was pushing it slowly and he was very gentle and patient but this was not what I wanted it to be. I kept thinking ouch, and it was cold. My panties looked like the beginning of my period tinged with pink when I woke up*

## MONTH SIX: SLEEPTALKING NAKED

*this morning. I guess, other than that, it wasn't good; it wasn't really bad. Maybe something is wrong with me. I wanted us to make love and I hope he never does it with anyone else in the whole world. I deserve to have him. I deserve to have just this one thing go right for me. I think if I didn't do it to him, he would do some other girl at his school. He's been a really good boyfriend so far and he's waited for me. He's been kind and even though I'm still not sure if I was ready for what happened yesterday, we have a lot of fun together. I am a little scared he's going to leave me now. I know sometimes they say after a guy has sex he doesn't want the girl he had sex with anymore. That's not Henry though. He's always treated me just fine.*

## MONTH SIX: SLEEPTALKING NAKED

I wasn't really ok, so I began to shake. I still didn't move or ask him to move; I just held on as he pumped inside of me more. The more he pumped, the more I pretended it didn't hurt until the pain was a growing throb, so uncomfortable I grabbed his forearm tightly. I thought about him leaving me after we'd made love, and I whispered to him:

"Promise me you'll never leave me, promise me you'll never leave me no matter what happens…"

"I won't leave you, no matter what," he muttered.

His fingertips grabbed my back as he pushed in and held himself there, as the rest of his body seemed to move in slow motion. I tightened every muscle I could feel. A few more tears streamed

## MONTH SIX: SLEEPTALKING NAKED

down, and I suddenly couldn't stop myself from breathing so heavily. What just happened? Did he?

I could smell a salty stale air, the smell of thick wetness. He grabbed me closer, and I tensed—my mind and body in collapse. Henry moved back slowly, and as he pulled out of me my whole body shook and I let go of the cries I'd been holding in. I pulled my sweats up quickly and fell over into his arms. He sat holding me closely in a hug. It began to drizzle.

****************************************************

I stared at the thick blood streaks on the toilet paper as I sat holding my stomach, staring at the dial tone, waiting for Mama to call back. I tried to remember to breathe. Try again. What if I was losing my baby? Would I die? Would he die? I looked at my

## MONTH SIX: SLEEPTALKING NAKED

stomach and peeled my underwear away from my abdomen and peeked inside. Blood. I balled my fists up on the counter, contemplating if I should call 911. Do you call 911 for something like this? I tried my mother again. As the phone rang, I thought about the way the phone kept ringing and ringing and ringing the night I called Henry to tell him the news of my pregnancy. I had the exact same pounding in my head after we'd had sex for the first time. The same feeling I had right now as my body slid to the floor under the counter, clenching the cordless phone. *Maybe I am not supposed to have this baby. Do I deserve to have a child anyway? I am too young, Henry doesn't love me, Daddy doesn't love me, and Mama doesn't have enough money to support us.* The phone rang and rang, and I tried Mama again. I got lost in my thoughts. I called and called Ma in a fury, just like the night I called Henry's house with the news of my pregnancy.

## MONTH SIX: SLEEPTALKING NAKED

\*\*\*

I had thought of not telling Henry anything, but I couldn't bear to get an abortion and not let him know. I'd called him that night, and I was leaning toward the decision to have an abortion. Daddy had set the appointment up already. Finally, Henry picked up the phone, and his family was arguing in the background.

"Henry. Hi, uhmm, can I talk to you?" I said in my crybaby voice. The voice I usually put on when I wanted someone to feel sorry for me. It generally worked.

"Yeah, wussup, man, wussup?" His tone brash and rushed. I was a girl, and today he called me a man.

## MONTH SIX: SLEEPTALKING NAKED

"You haven't called me back," I said. "What's going on? I miss you."

"Yeah, I've been busy."

"Henry, I'm pregnant." The phone line went so quiet I thought he didn't hear me. "Hello? Hello?"

"Whatchoo gon' do?"

"What am I gonna do? Don't you mean what are *we* gonna do?"

"Man, I ono. I made my bed, now I'm-a lay in it I guess." Henry spoke calmly.

I was so disappointed I was shocked into silence.

## MONTH SIX: SLEEPTALKING NAKED

He hadn't spoken to me but briefly since we made love. I began to worry whether Henry ever really put the condom on in the first place. I asked Henry if he could tell his mom and dad I was pregnant, and he said he would and quickly hung up. I felt they should know. Everyone should know what he'd done to me! I felt myself outside of myself, watching as I hit redial over and over again until the machine picked up. Again, I'd try again. I heard someone pick up and then slam the phone down. That was when I realized he was trying to make sure I didn't tell his parents I was pregnant with his baby. I waited a few hours and it was well after midnight. Suddenly the feeling I had wouldn't let me believe in anything he'd said. When I called, Henry's mother picked up with a tired voice. All I could do was cry. I handed my mother the phone as she sat next to me, her hand resting on my knee.

MONTH SIX: SLEEPTALKING NAKED

"Hello, is this Henry's mother? Mrs. Black?"

"Yes, it is. Can I help you with something?"

"My daughter, Lalanii, and Henry, they've been together, and my daughter is pregnant with your son's baby."

My body felt faint and numb.

My mother handed me the phone. I tried to listen as Henry's mother tried to bond with me by asking questions I couldn't answer.

"How did this happen? What are you going to do?"

I responded to her in my head: *What am I going to do, bitch? What about what are* we *going to do?*

## MONTH SIX: SLEEPTALKING NAKED

"Well, I am here for you if you need me or if you need anything…
… …"

*I need this reversed. I need your son to be supportive and for you to stop asking me dumb-ass questions. I need you to not feel like a fake-ass piece of cake with snot in the middle. What am I going to do, bitch? Shut the fuck up.*

The rest of her words trailed off. I cried into the phone; her calm exterior was a complete sham. I more than suspected something was wrong. I knew for certain.

All I could think about was the way Henry said he'd told his mother, and he really hadn't. He had really just gone to sleep. How could he have just hung up on me and gone to sleep?

## MONTH SIX: SLEEPTALKING NAKED

\*\*\*

He definitely had a part in creating this child, and now he got to just rest easy on his pillow-top mattress? Not possible. There was no way I'd be ok with the idea that he got my treasure, and the memory of him being the first man who had ever gone inside of me would be all I had to show for it. I could feel anger glowing in my blood. Since I couldn't hurt him physically, I'd keep his son and persevere beyond him. I'd have my baby because he didn't have the decency to love me enough, to simply call me back and have a conversation. I wasn't worth a few minutes to him. I'd have my son to fill the void his dad couldn't. There was no way I wouldn't hold on to him while at the same time keep him away from me. It wasn't okay that we contributed equally to this, but I got the brunt of the pain that comes with having to make a choice

## MONTH SIX: SLEEPTALKING NAKED

to have an abortion, give my child up for adoption, or raise my child in harsh conditions. But, I decided, I could go it alone. I could raise my child completely, with or without his help. I'd have my son because he was my choice. My. Mine.

*Dear diary,*

*I remember when Henry told me once when we were sleeptalking that he wanted to marry me and have children one day. He told me he wanted a boy and a girl and if we made love and I got pregnant, he would take care of his child and take care of me. He was so sure when he said it, I was reassured of the person he was. I never thought about pregnancy, but I always fantasized about marriage. Later, he explained how much he loved me in metaphor. He told me he loved me bigger than the*

MONTH SIX: SLEEPTALKING NAKED

*biggest clouds in the largest sky. I love when he says stuff like this! Then he told me he loved me more than I loved to write in my diary. Henry never calls me anymore, he keeps promising to call me and he never does. Words are all we have, and I don't believe his words anymore.*

Henry and I walked back to the apartment holding each other. His eyes kept saying *I love you are you ok*. I was in so much shock I tried not to look at him. I felt closer to him, and I didn't regret anything. He walked me to the top of the stairs, and my mom opened the door on us as I was taking out my key. *Great*, I thought.

"Where y'all two lovebirds been? And you know it's eleven o'clock, Henry, where are your parents? Are they on the way? And your homework better be finished, lil' girl."

## MONTH SIX: SLEEPTALKING NAKED

I nodded a yes, never looking up.

"Ashley is picking me up in a few minutes," Henry said without looking at my mother.

"Alright, well I'm gon' go on to bed. Ohh, them folks at work stress me out so badly." Mom's voice faded off as she closed the door to her room.

We fell into silence, and a few minutes later, I heard Ashley's car pull up. I hadn't heard Henry call him, but I heard his car and him fooling around outside on the phone. Henry looked at me, said, "I love you," and held my hand longer than usual before letting go. I stared at the crease in his pants as he walked out of the door. I followed him out into the hallway, then watched him through the window, staring at his white jacket with blue trim. I waved at

## MONTH SIX: SLEEPTALKING NAKED

Ashley, and he winked, I could tell they were talking about me. I felt a low drop in my stomach; it was pounding.

\*\*\*

When I woke up, I was no longer crunched under the counter on the floor staring at the cordless phone waiting for my mother to come back. I was lying across the black couch, covered in my favorite fluffy lion blanket. I looked over at some soup—steam coming from the bowl. Ma was home.

"When it cools off, you should eat. Why were you on the floor, honey? And my phone was dead. Are you ok?"

## MONTH SIX: SLEEPTALKING NAKED

I felt my stomach. My heartbeat hopscotched; I rushed my hands to my panties to feel for wetness. There was no wetness. I closed my eyes. I stood up slowly and walked to the bathroom. *Please make my baby ok. Please don't let him die.*

I took a breath, and normal urine trickled out. I wiped myself and studied the tissue. With the tissue in my left hand, I turned on the shower water with my right. As I ran the warm water into hot, I felt my bulge and wished Henry could feel it too. How did I ever even consider an abortion? Not only did I love the baby growing inside of me, I loved that Henry would pay for not calling me and for not loving me anymore. I had a new best friend now: my baby. I looked down at the tissue, and there was no blood. The streaks of blood in my panties had dried.

# MONTH SEVEN:

# DADDY DOESN'T DANCE

### DADDY'S LITTLE WORLD PART I: MEMORIES

Daddy's little girl is growing a world inside her. Yes, I am running running running over. I am remembering. I am probably six or seven. I am remembering Daddy's forehead scrunched up as we laughed over my hot chocolate and I pretended it was coffee—like his. My eyes are glazed over in adoration, my hands playing in Daddy's beard. I am studying Daddy's tone and intelligent words, his mannerisms. And then, I am here. I have

## MONTH SEVEN: DADDY DOESN'T DANCE

turned sixteen, and I have a whole belly full of Pregnorant now. I spoke to my cousin Toni-Ann and got enraged. She reported to me that Daddy had staged a makeshift funeral for me and told the rest of his side of the family I had passed away.

### DADDY DOESN'T DANCE

I remembered being maybe thirteen-fourteenish, sitting under the kitchen table gripping the center pole, waiting for Mama to say something juicy. The pink swirly floor was cool, and I got to eavesdrop on plenty of conversations. That afternoon, I sat with my cheeks puffed out, hand over my face, as she gushed to her friend about how things had changed in her life seven or so years before when she'd fallen in love with a man who wasn't my daddy.

## MONTH SEVEN: DADDY DOESN'T DANCE

A man she met on a night when she'd gone out with my daddy. I overheard it was on that same night that Daddy had a bum knee from falling off a ladder while trying to put up a sign. Daddy wasn't a great dancer anyway.

"Get on up, ole man, and dance with your woman!" I imagined Ma roared.

"Nawhh, honey, there's plenty a' gentlemen that'll show you a dance or two, go 'head," I know Daddy replied. And so she did. A short man with a patch of gray in the front of his hair winked at her like she was Whitney Houston when she sang, "I Wanna Dance with Somebody." The man with whom she danced, she began a seven-year affair with.

## MONTH SEVEN: DADDY DOESN'T DANCE

### FRIED TURKEY JERK

One Thanksgiving morning not long after that, I sat shaking my head under that same kitchen island table, one hand squeezing the pole. Ma sent Dad on a wild chase for peanut oil so she could fry up a turkey. Why she'd waited until the "thanking morning" to do so was beyond me, but this was the case. Daddy finally found tiny bottles of $3.99 oil at the only department store open on that morning. He complained of how expensive it was and how much more of it he could've gotten for less had it not been Thanksgiving and piss-poor planning.

Ma hummed and switched her hips in the kitchen, gathering the rest of the dinner. Dad had angrily bought out the entire supply of oil as it was a large turkey, and what Mama wanted, Daddy always made sure he supplied. When he returned, he must have snuck

## MONTH SEVEN: DADDY DOESN'T DANCE

through quietly. I later understood that it was at that moment when he'd picked up the phone to check if he'd have to go into his office. It was that moment on that day that he'd picked up the phone, and the phone was already speed-dialing another number that had been programmed in. I suppose he'd expected to hear me snickering and he'd playfully scold, or he'd expected one of Mama's loud family members. Instead, he heard:

"Hi, baby, he's still here, but he'll be leaving in a few minutes."

"Can't wait to taste some of that fried turkey babeeeey!"

Dad overheard the plans of his cheating never-been wife and paced the house, preparing the turkey fryer. Since it took two people to hoist the turkey in and again out of the scalding-hot oil, Dad was careful not to let go. Every muscle in his body must have gone

## MONTH SEVEN: DADDY DOESN'T DANCE

tense and solid, knowing what he knew then—every emotion pulsing, desperately trying to hang on to the wire hanger to lower the turkey into the fryer without splashing. Even after having bought out the entire supply of peanut oil, he had to add a bit of vegetable oil because, still, it was not enough.

### INSPECTOR GADGET

Because of Dad's status and experience in the military, he knew how to make two calls and find out every deep and dark secret any person ever had. Dad had a private investigator take pictures, video clips, and even voice recordings of Ma's rendezvous as soon as the very next day.

MONTH SEVEN: DADDY DOESN'T DANCE

\*

She was driving her fancy new purple Camry Prism with gold trim he'd purchased for her not too long before. In some pictures, she was coming out of the Snooty Fox Motel with Mr. Ze, and in her hands she held her cooler—in it, her Miller Lite beer and a plate of the turkey she'd made us for Thanksgiving dinner the night before. He had proof of the kissing and the hugging, and he even found Mr. Ze was already married and his wife was dying of lymphoma or leukemia (I cannot remember which).

\*

When I begin to understand all of this, I am stopped to my very core. I feel red-orange rage at Mama. At Daddy for never coming home on time. At myself for being Pregnorant. When I call Daddy,

## MONTH SEVEN: DADDY DOESN'T DANCE

he will not speak to me. It is likely he thinks I have chosen a side. Usually my father is the type of man who will talk to me about anything. This time, he answers the phone, breathes, and then hangs up. When I first remember finding out about Mama's affair, I sharply remember the crack in his voice, the shake in his tone, and the almost visible break of his heart into tiny porcelain and gold-trimmed pieces.

The memory is so fresh in my mind, but so long ago. Today, I am Daddy's little girl, patting and caressing my belly, Daddy's big girl with a world in her belly.

## MONTH SEVEN: DADDY DOESN'T DANCE

### CHECK UN-MATE

A few years before my pregnancy—but not too long before Ma's tiptoe was discovered—I was hiding in Dad's darkroom at his graphics company, SignXPress. I found the name of his company ironic because the very reason his company went under was because people could produce a similar product *faster*. Anyway, I was almost a teenager, so I wanted to be left alone. It was red inside and quiet. Opposite that room was his camera room, and adjacent was a large mirror tilting sideways against his silkscreen glass table. I saw Dad through the mirror as he spoke to a skinny guy with shoulder-length hair who looked as pale as a vanilla latté; he worked in the back of the shop. Daddy stared down at the paint-splashed floor as he confided in his employee that he'd suspected Mama was only cashing the checks that could be deposited into

## MONTH SEVEN: DADDY DOESN'T DANCE

their joint account together, the checks that had Dad's name. The checks written to the company's name had gone missing. Thousands of dollars.

\*

Daddy then told him that he was sure he was upside-down on his payments because he'd entrusted Ma to deposit them all. It must have been too much trouble to deposit the others. Dad leaned on the wall-sized easel as he shook his head; he looked as though he were choking, his eyes sunken in, his face in an eerie tinge, almost bluish. Months later, Daddy discovered, in a top drawer in our kitchen, all of the checks written to his company without his name. The checks were dated months earlier and could no longer be cashed. Dad thought Ma had cashed all of his checks, but she'd

MONTH SEVEN: DADDY DOESN'T DANCE

only cashed **and/or** deposited the money she could spend. The rest of the expired checks still sat in the drawer.

## BLUE IN THE FACE

Dad told me when I was about five Mama had taken me to visit him at his shop like usual, and as usual I ate all of the taffy and peppermint rounds that sat in the wide crystal bowl hidden at his desk for his customers. I vaguely remember discovering the taste of the green and the pink round mints, and figuring out those colors were sweet instead of minty. He told me I'd popped a green peppermint round in my mouth and was twiddling my fingers, trying to grab every Pilot Precise ink pen I could find. I was exactly one head taller than his silkscreen glass-top table, and as

## MONTH SEVEN: DADDY DOESN'T DANCE

I'd leaned my head back in utter glee, the green round got caught in my throat. I ran to Dad, thrashing and flinging my hands back and forth and gripping my neckline. He panicked. He and Ma immediately turned me upside-down, shaking me by one tennis shoe, Ma screaming with tears in her eyes, Dad determined. They had teamwork, but I was still getting blue.

My arms wilted as Mama frantically tried to pry fingers into my throat, my eyes entreating. Warren, my sister's almost-husband at the time, ran in, swept me up into his arms, and did a vigorous Heimlich maneuver. With one sharp thrust, the peppermint round shot out across the floor. My body went limp, my eyes stuck in purple circles, deprived of oxygen.

MONTH SEVEN: DADDY DOESN'T DANCE

*

Dad said that day was the scariest day of his life. But for me, looking at him from behind the door on the floor in the darkroom, his body needing to lean against the easel just to stand—he was the one choking; his face permanently sunk. Shortly after this occasion, he had to pack up his entire business and move it to our home, and that was like making space when there was no space.

**FISHIES**

After I decided to stay pregnant, all I had at that point was memories. From the time I was a child and throughout my teenage years, my family went to Mountain Lakes Vacation Resort. It was a time-share in the mountains—about a day's driving distance, it had

## MONTH SEVEN: DADDY DOESN'T DANCE

always seemed to me. I fuzzily recall the first time I saw snow, but I clearly recall the first time I went fishing. I was seven, and Daddy was fussing at me for not sitting there quiet enough for the fish to bite my hook. I was trying to tell him I felt something tugging, that I felt a slight pull. He didn't believe me, so I started reeling my line in very slowly because I knew he'd have been mad to see me "playing" with it again. He looked over at me with fury in his eyes, and I swung my pole out of the water as everyone around us ducked down or leaned back. An audience of fishermen stared, as did Daddy, their mouths open wide as I screamed and jumped.

"I caught it, Daddieee! I caught a fishie!" Daddy laughed so big and so proud his anger went away, and his habitually knotted angry eyebrows took the day off. He kept praising me for catching that fish, kept praising me all day long. All I wanted to do was make

## MONTH SEVEN: DADDY DOESN'T DANCE

him happy, all I ever wanted was for him to be happy, for Daddy to be happy for me.

That same night Daddy, brought all of our fishies home to the cabin. I thought since my fish was a baby, I'd keep her and put her in a tank. While Dad and his friend Kaden—Beatrice's lover who lived beneath my sister in the back apartment—weren't looking, I fed my newly caught fish, Sadie, water from my My Little Pony cup. She looked like she had rainbows on her scales, and her fins made her look like she could fly. I was in love with her so much I fed her mom in the ice chest too, then I fed all of the fishies so much water back and forth until they started to gobble. Their mouths started to suck air and they began to flipper slightly. After over an hour or so they began to move vigorously in the chest, skittering around like they'd come back to life.

## MONTH SEVEN: DADDY DOESN'T DANCE

\*

I was just going to tell Daddy how much happier they were with me looking after them when Dad took Sadie by her neck and chopped her head clean off into the sink. I burst into tears, and Dad and Kaden continued cutting every one of those catfish up. I ran to my bunk and hunched over, hugging my legs and pillow as tight as I could. I could not understand why Dad was so mean to catch them if he was only going to cut their heads off. I felt the same way today, seven months full, that I felt that day, except when I tried to grab my knees to pull them to my stomach to a crouched position, I could not reach. My body was too big. I remember being so angry he'd decapitated my fishies; I remember he just smiled and explained to me that it was the circle of life or something ridiculous like that.

## MONTH SEVEN: DADDY DOESN'T DANCE

\*

I wanted to tell Dad that having this baby was just a circle of life and as ridiculous as that sounded, I would do the best I could. But when I called every day from the day I found out I was having a boy child, Daddy wouldn't speak to me.

### SNEAKILY

Sometimes when we lived in the old house with the brick steps, I would pick up the house phone and Ma would be talking to her insurance agent lover. I always figured it was just one of her friends, but I wasn't entirely sure. Once I caught on, I started listening on the other receiver. I listened all the time and heard her

## MONTH SEVEN: DADDY DOESN'T DANCE

conversations so much for a long while I couldn't hear any other voice from her besides that sneaky little voice.

Daddy was profusely fascinated with art agonizinig over being better than anyone and having completed work he was proud of, rather than finishing on time. Dad was profusely brilliant in what he did, but often he could not see outside of what he did. Nonetheless, there was no justification for Mama steaming crab legs, broccoli, and potatoes for Daddy while whispering, "I love you," to Mr. Ze on most nights. I knew when Ma was talking to her secret agent lover because her face lit up like Vegas on the Fourth of July. Her head curved against the cordless phone scrunched between her neck and shoulder.

## MONTH SEVEN: DADDY DOESN'T DANCE

**CRASHED**

After the business had to be brought home, Daddy also was set to lose our house in Culver City. He'd often speak to me like he was set to explode any moment from his bitterness. And he rambled. He ended up getting out of that house and into something else far less desirable, but still a very beautiful area. Huge, six-room corner house, big and white with wall-to-wall windows spread along the main room, Hawaiian décor in the bar room, and a full backyard as well as front. He called Mama the "two-million-dollar woman," joking that two million dollars was what she'd cost him. Mama said Dad specifically asked her not to work after having me. I am not sure requests like that have an expiration date, but if so, Ma

## MONTH SEVEN: DADDY DOESN'T DANCE

was well beyond the curdle stage. Daddy was understaffed at work and wasn't providing service quick enough—because he couldn't find anyone he trusted—which made his turnaround time slower. The competition began to beat Daddy into a steel box with a lid. He didn't change with the digital age, and you could say he walked around only half alive.

\*

Mama ran right into a truck one day not long after and crashed her purple Camry Prism with gold trim. It was totaled, but she walked away with only a stiff back, fully at fault. Mama moved to the new house on the corner with us but barely stayed six months before Dad couldn't pretend anymore. I was pregnant less than a year after she left.

## MONTH SEVEN: DADDY DOESN'T DANCE

I guess Dad finally refused to keep painting over a mucked canvas. He confronted her one night about her affair, with proof and pictures. Ma was drinking as usual when she flared and ran through the house on a binge of "I don't give a fuck." When she reached the back of the house, Daddy flew behind her, trying to catch the door from slamming, but the metal-heavy wood door crashed into his forearm, slicing meat from his arm, opening full gushes of red.

\*

Dad wrapped his bloody arm and quickly drove himself to the hospital. When he got there, half-hunched over, he told me the nurses explained it was an "otherworldly type of miracle" he'd even made it to the hospital after losing so much blood. Pieces of the window glass had to be picked out of his arm. The

## MONTH SEVEN: DADDY DOESN'T DANCE

housekeeper, Martha, saw the whole ordeal and called the police on Mama as she sped off down Rodeo to the condo my sister had moved to with her husband. Mama was speed-driving a borrowed green Honda given to her by her niece after her accident. The police pulled her over after following her inside the private community. They arrested her without allowing her to make a call to her daughter, who was just right up the stairs. Ma told me that despite how loud she was, no one heard her through the window, and she saw her whole world crash down in front of her in a flash as she was charged with a DUI. That Friday night, no one posted her bail, and she spent the weekend in jail.

MONTH SEVEN: DADDY DOESN'T DANCE

**OLDER AND OLDER AND COLDER**

When Ma came to get her clothes from Dad's, she was still asking if Dad had heard from the insurance company about replacing her totaled car. Dad had heard from the insurance company all right, and he told me that he and his own insurance agent had "laughed her cheating ass right to the bank." The money for her new car was deposited into Dad's account; soon after, he changed the locks on her. At this time, I was visiting Ma at my sister's, only on weekends.

\*

I'd met Henry that next summer. Being with him counteracted the loss of my favorite home in downtown Culver City and Ma not living at home anymore. The new house was big, old, cold, and

## MONTH SEVEN: DADDY DOESN'T DANCE

haunted. I was told the old lady who'd lived there before us had white hair and an infinite number of cats, and she'd died in my room. It wasn't my old house with the swivel staircase and brick front steps. Daddy got grumpier every day. No more fishing trips with tackle boxes and hooks and flying neon gadgets to play with. Daddy's Santa belly got bigger. Mama was out and in love, and no one was getting on her case.

*

People like to tell you the relationship with your parents is what matters most growing up. Your friendships within your lifestyle. The experiences you grow from. Self-help seminars like to promise you it's best you pay the most attention to yourself and how you make yourself happy, or else it'll inform every decision you make. But it's not only a mix of all of those things; more often than not,

## MONTH SEVEN: DADDY DOESN'T DANCE

it's just accountability. If Dad and Mama could have taken accountability for the villains they became to each other, they, as well as I, might have lived a more fulfilling youth. We are all learning, and not only are we all not perfect, but most of us are fairly neurotic, extremely fearful, and often insecure. It's not easy to fix because we all grew into it, just like growing up.

\*

### SPANKING

That was the same summer Daddy spanked me. It was right before I met Henry. My friend Esther and I were hot to trot and trying to meet boys who had cars to take us places. We wanted to live wildly, and we wanted to see every bit of LA. Together we concocted a plan that she'd get dropped off by her parents as

## MONTH SEVEN: DADDY DOESN'T DANCE

quietly as she could, and I'd see her through the window and wave good-bye to Dad, pretending her parents were picking us up. Some cute guy she'd met would grab us from the McDonald's a block away and we'd be off on our little adventure. I did as we'd planned. We began to walk down Rodeo toward La Brea, singing the raunchy lyrics to Lil' Kim's "Not Tonight."

\*

Daddy must have intercepted our plans somehow because about five minutes after we'd arrived at the McDonald's parking lot, Dad's Land Cruiser raced up and double-parked across three lanes. He jumped out high on adrenaline and anger and grabbed my arm, then started whacking me awkwardly, sporadically. I hopped up and down like I was playing gimpy hopscotch. Esther was yelled at and told to get in, and her parents called to pick her back up. Two

## MONTH SEVEN: DADDY DOESN'T DANCE

weeks later, I met Henry. I never wanted to see another guy in any car or sneak out of the house ever again. All I wanted was for him to sneak in—and hold me, hold me until I fell asleep.

### DADDY'S LITTLE WORLD PART II: A CONVERSATION

"Daaaaaddy, say something, Daddy Daddy, it's me, Lalanii, please, say hello, all I hear is silence—I'm going to keep talking. I've called you so many times and you never answer, Daddy, I have so much to tell you, I miss you so much, Dad, my body is getting so much bigger, Daddy, and I'm learning so much, Daddy, Mama took me to the DMV last Thursday, wait, Daddy, I have to tell you all about it, I have never been so afraid in my entire life, my future and my baby's future was dependent on whether or not I got my permit and it was so crazy when I went in the DMV I had to stand in this long line even though I had an appointment and

## MONTH SEVEN: DADDY DOESN'T DANCE

there was this old wrinkly woman in a raspberry hat who kept coughing right on my neck, and she saw I was pregnant!"

"...Daddy, are you there?"

*

Daddy had answered his home phone but hadn't said a word. I was two months away from giving birth, and I wanted, needed, to tell him every solitary thing I felt. I suppose he just wanted to listen, or he was so incensed he didn't have anything to say, but I'd take that, I'd take silence over nothing. I'd take silence over him not answering the phone at all. I'd been speaking to his answering machine for weeks.

*

MONTH SEVEN: DADDY DOESN'T DANCE

**DMV**

"Daddy, it was so horrible," I continued on, "so I just stood there and I was thinking they were going to give me the written test or something easy like that—but they took me to the side and, Dad, I really forgot to review all of the information in my test booklet, and when I got outside, it was pouring down like the Nāmaka\* (Hawaiian rain goddess) was trying to drown out a kingdom! I was so nervous, and the instructor was not friendly, Daddy, she looked like my third grade math teacher Dr. Perkins, and she had the same flumpy cheeks but she had brown skin and a big black rain poncho and rain boots to match and she had a Budweiser umbrella, who has a Budweiser umbrella at the DMV?"

\*

## MONTH SEVEN: DADDY DOESN'T DANCE

"So, Daddy, that made me nervous, so when she motioned to get in the car I went toward the passenger seat and she shook her head in annoyance. 'We are going to see if you can drive,' she said. And what witchery she was, so I got in and tried to look around for any traffic and check my mirrors and I heard her mumble something about me not checking my back mirror, then I saw her write something down so I started frowning and crying in my heart, then I pulled off in a slight jerking motion and decided not to care whether I passed or failed because it looked like I'd failed already, and as I was driving I was thinking of all of the times I'd driven Mom's car as practice to work, almost every day to school and other places, Daddy, I'd been driving a lot, really, a lot, Dad."

\*

MONTH SEVEN: DADDY DOESN'T DANCE

"So we drove around the Inglewood DMV, near something that looked like a park, and the windshield wipers were so messed up, Daddy, it was so embarrassing they started squeaking like a juicy fart bubble across the glass and I just wanted to die and I saw the lady smile, Daddy, she was *laughing* at me, so I drove more careless, I checked where I was going, but I calmed down and pretended I was ignoring her, stupid math-teacher-look-alike lady, she was so dumb, Dad, then she kept asking me to go in circles, then she told me to make a U-turn and, then I hesitated.

"'But the sign says no U-turns.'

"'Ok, then just turn left up here.'

"'But we just came from that way.'

## MONTH SEVEN: DADDY DOESN'T DANCE

"Then, Daddy, she rolls her stupid eyes at me like an idiot, and tells me to go up to the next light and then she tells me to pass this old beat-up purple Toyota like Mama used to have, Dad, so I felt like I should pass it because it was old and beat up and I hated that Toyota, so I did, I looked behind in my blind spot like I was taught, and just as a heavier gush of rain came down, I sped up to pass the car. The second I did so, the lady asked me to pull over to the side and get out of the car, I asked her if I'd done anything wrong because she seemed agitated and she didn't answer, and I started to panic."

\*

"*My mom and I drive every morning! She's in the car with me! She knows I can drive, I may have made a mistake or something, but I can drive, and I'm seven months pregnant and my baby will*

## MONTH SEVEN: DADDY DOESN'T DANCE

*need diapers and formula and I will need a license and I will need one now, not in thirty days when I have to retake this stupid test, you know I can drive, and I know you know, and you've been mean to me ever since you sat in this car and you could've smiled once or not tried to give me mixed messages or trick me, you're just not being fair!'* Yes, Dad, I screamed at the DMV lady."

\*

The lady's face was unchanged, and my emotion seemed to go unnoticed, my head hot. She pulled up at the front of the DMV and got out of the car. Ma was waiting outside having a beer; I could see her in the distance. I got out of the car, my lips pressed tight, my tears not able to strike any longer. I burst into tears at the moment the lady looked at me and said,

## MONTH SEVEN: DADDY DOESN'T DANCE

"Never pass a slower car to get over in front of them in the rain. *You've passed.*" Her monotone voice made me strain to hear what I knew I'd heard.

"And, Daddy, can you believe it? I passed, I passed, Daddy, I passed!!" The phone hung up.

"Daddy... Daddy?"

\*

I called back several times, to no avail.

I tried back several more times and got no answer. No answer the next day, or the next. I was determined. I waited a week and then called again and left a message telling him I would try back in the night. When I called back later, the phone picked up, I began my spiel.

## MONTH SEVEN: DADDY DOESN'T DANCE

### DADDY, WHAT'S WRONG WITH YOU?

"Daddy, you haven't answered in a week! What is wrong with you! It's a shame I talk to you and you won't speak back to me. Are you even listening? Every time I call you back, if you answer you seem to listen to me longer, which has got to be a good sign. I can hear you breathing. Daddy, I didn't mean to hurt you when I left you in the clinic that day and when you waited for me those weeks after school in your car, I wanted to come to the car, Daddy, but I just couldn't. Daddy, I have a little world in my stomach, and I am going to love him, I am going to love him so big and hard and wide. I am going to love him, but, Daddy, please don't stop loving me." *Click* went the phone into the receiver. I held the phone so long the dial tone lady told me if I would like to make a call, to please hang up and try again. And that is what I did.

## MONTH SEVEN: DADDY DOESN'T DANCE

### BROKER THAN A JOKER

"Daddy, I know it's been a few days since I've called you, but Mama is making me do all of this housework and it's killing me! She is making me do all of the stuff around the house that she's too lazy to do, matching up her socks, and her dishes, and cleaning up the living room even if I'm not the one to dirty it up, she even had me clean the mirrors and spray the windows with Windex and wipe them, she's punishing me or something, the mirrors and windows never get cleaned!"

\*

"And my body is so heavy, my breasts are so big, and Henry's family won't help with any money. Mama called yesterday and they want nothing to do with us when it comes down to money,

## MONTH SEVEN: DADDY DOESN'T DANCE

they say they'll call back and they never do, then Mama gets mad at me and says to me I need to take my a-s-s down to the county building and get some financial assistance, and I hear her talking on the phone now, Daddy, she's talking about me like I'm not even here! She's telling people we're broke, but if we have no money, the last thing I want people to know is we have no money! The other day I finally called Henry's house myself, I got so fed up with being in the middle."


"Hi, Mrs. Black, it's Lalanii."

"Hi, Lalanuuuh, how are you?" Henry's mother mispronouncing my name like I hate so much.

## MONTH SEVEN: DADDY DOESN'T DANCE

"I'm ok, I wanted to talk to you about if you had any extra money because I need to replace bras and panties that no longer fit, and my Ma, she's a little strapped for cash."

"Well, honey, that's just not something we will be able to help with. Now, once the baby is here we will do what we can, but this was one of the reasons I tried to steer you from making this decision…" Shiree's tone sounds as though she's sitting on her high throne, thinking up *I told you so's.*

\*

Her voice trailed off again like Charlie Brown's mother, unintelligible and not anything I wanted to hear. "Daddy, I can't believe these people, that's why I really need you to support me, be there for me, no one else is in my corner, I have no friends who

## MONTH SEVEN: DADDY DOESN'T DANCE

call, I have no family who care beyond curiosity, I need you, Daddy, please, please? I love you, Daddy."

Daddy hung up. I called back, again, and I called and called. No answer. And that was all of the listening I would get for the day.

### THERE IS HOPE AND THEN THERE IS NOT

"Daddy, bottom line is, you work too much, and that didn't justify anything, but I would always wait for you to get home all of the time and give me some type of attention, and you never would, you'd come home too late and be too tired and life goes along, and you would miss it, all of it, and I don't want you to miss a thing, not one single moment, nothing, I want you to see my baby and be a part of our lives, and, Dad, I'm strong, I'm studying and haven't

## MONTH SEVEN: DADDY DOESN'T DANCE

missed very many classes even though I'm sluggish and have gotten really fat. I got a job, Dad, I got a job! I'm an artist like you, I'm painting a mural along the Ballona Creek, in the neighborhood, it's a work-study program, but I get paid minimum wage for it."

\*

"It makes me happy and feel good, I feel good every day when I do it, they allow me to wear my headphones while I paint and, Dad, they made me in charge of the others in my group, and I'm saving every penny and so far I have four hundred dollars in emergency money, Daddy, Mama cries at night over money, and she doesn't know, I can overhear her phone conversations, she acts as though I'm not here when she says all of her grown-up stuff, and, Dad, I had no idea that you and Ma were together thirty years but never legally got married—why not, Dad? How come you never married Mama?" The phone

## MONTH SEVEN: DADDY DOESN'T DANCE

slammed in my ear. The second I heard the phone hang up, I wished I hadn't said it. After that, Dad wouldn't answer for weeks and weeks.

### A BOY BABY

Finally he picked up. I was overjoyed! "Daddy, Daddy, I'm sorry, please, please, I'm sorry, at the doctor appointment they finally confirmed I am having a boy, can you believe it, Daddy?"

Daddy sighed heavily.

"I knew it, I am having a boy! They couldn't tell on every picture for sure, but it is confirmed, he is a boy. He moves a lot now and at first I thought it was just gas bubbles, but, Dadddddy, he moves! I dreamt he's going to look just like you, Daddy, he swims in my stomach and when I hold my belly I swear he can feel me, and

## MONTH SEVEN: DADDY DOESN'T DANCE

sometimes he even pushes back! I'm naming him after you, Daddddy, he'll be the most beautiful baby in the world!"

The phone rustled, the tone of voice was cold, distant, and spiritless, barely resembling my father. He spoke eight words I will never forget as long as I live.

"I do not know you. Good day, ma'am."

I listened as my father spoke to me as if I were a stranger. My blood rushed. Veins pulsated as I pressed the receiver down into the cradle as if it were going to explode. I shrugged my shoulders and stepped back from the phone. Then I snatched the phone up again and threw it against the wall and it crashed apart, the colorful wires sprouting out of the battery pack. That cordless phone never worked that well anyway.

# MONTH EIGHT:

# LET'S JUST HAVE THE BABY SHOWER

# AT THE WELFARE OFFICE... OR

### Absent Parent Questionnaire

As a condition of eligibility for CA, you are required by law to provide information about the absent parent of the children receiving assistance. YOU MUST ANSWER EVERY QUESTION.

## 1. What is the name of the absent parent?

Henry Walter Black II.

## MONTH EIGHT: ABSENT PARENT QUESTIONNAIRE

Mom says we have no money, and because of this I have to go to the welfare office and complete the filing against Henry so I can get money from the County. I am sitting at my baby shower amazed at all of the surroundings, thinking about what I wrote on my welfare paperwork last month.

**2. What is the absent parent's Social Security number—from his/her pay stubs, tax returns, bank loans, old ID cards, or official papers?**

How would I know? I'm having a hard time remembering my own. Pay stub? Tax return? That sounds like stuff I've heard my parents say.

MONTH EIGHT: ABSENT PARENT QUESTIONNAIRE

**3. What is the status of the relationship between the custodial and absentee parent? If married, please include date of marriage and copy of marriage certificate:**

Not sure what the status is since his untimely abomination. I mean, since he left. I was once a lovely flower; I am now a soon-blossoming blob.

**4. Date of marriage:**

Yeah, right. Marriage is a wishful thought I had (thought and flunked) once.

MONTH EIGHT: ABSENT PARENT

QUESTIONNAIRE

## 5. Are you, or were you ever legally married to this absent parent?

Well, I'd planned on it eventually, but apparently Henry had other plans that included promising things he wouldn't deliver on (though he was perfectly capable.)

## 6. Are you legally separated from this absent parent?

I don't know what you mean by legally separated, but we sleep separately even though I'm carrying his almost-finished-baking baby and we'd dated each other for quite some time before my conception of this ginormous bowling ball.

## 7. Are you legally divorced from this absent parent?

## MONTH EIGHT: ABSENT PARENT QUESTIONNAIRE

If we'd been married, the stars would've aligned. Or better, the stars would have given me a false alarm and it would have been a negative pregnancy test result. This is just my bad luck because I have no means to support my baby. But I chose to have this baby, so I have to get it together.

## 8. When did you last see the absent parent?

I am looking dead in his face right this instant. He is going to tell me a few lies, and I am going to live and then later write this scene:

Early in the morning the day of the shower, my cousins came over to help set up. Roxanne, Ia, and Wanda tied "It's a boy!" décor to the centerpieces, taped secret notes to the bottoms of the chairs people were going to sit on, and organized a collection of music,

## MONTH EIGHT: ABSENT PARENT QUESTIONNAIRE

games and gifts. There'd been invitations, but mainly people just came because they wanted to know how big of a cow I was now. I could see the headlines:

*Sixteen-year-old has baby shower at Rec Center in*

*Cameo Woods, Everybody come on down! Baby having baby!!*

I am a shamed spectacle. I'm not myself at all, and I want all of this over. I force a smile.

When I came downstairs to take my first look at the Recreation Center where the shower would be held, I wanted to cry. This was really happening. The space was wide open, the table covers pale

## MONTH EIGHT: ABSENT PARENT QUESTIONNAIRE

yellow, white, and sky blue. The room, smelled of lemon cake and vanilla buttercream frosting and helium.

The balloons matched. Streamers and curlicued ribbons hung from the ceiling. The peach vertical blinds accentuated the baby shower theme. In the top right corner of the room, a table held presents. A single large gift sat atop the table. The table on the left was for the cake, which was covered. The table was strewn with confetti-paper baby boys, white paper plates, sky blue–trimmed napkins, and a complete matching set of pastel utensils.

The cake was made by my mom's closest friend, Carol. Carol was redheaded, freckled, high-energy, witty; I considered her my second mother. There was a Bundt cake. It looked odd as yellow glaze oozed delicately down its side.

## MONTH EIGHT: ABSENT PARENT QUESTIONNAIRE

My belly and I wore an Adidas shirt in light blue, brand-new all-white Adidas I specifically bought with my savings money the day before, and light blue and white Adidas snap-button track pants. I figured I had to get in the habit; I was housing a baby boy. That's a lie—there wasn't anything else in the closet that fit me.

I picked a flower and put it in my hair after remembering that Henry and I once walked around the complex and found the foyer covered in what seemed like flowering vines. He'd picked a fuchsia-and-yellow flower and placed it in my hair behind my ear.

People began to arrive. Lots of people. I noticed them by smell first. Heavy perfume, ughhh too much cologne, owweeee old lady scent, bleh—Victoria's Secret Love Spell body spray. It was overwhelming. I talked about pregnancy woes with a few family

## MONTH EIGHT: ABSENT PARENT QUESTIONNAIRE

members, and I was about to let them see my stomach, helping them to hold my shirt up below my breasts in order to have an accurate measurement for the guessing game, when Henry walked in like he could float on his own bullshit.

## 9. Where did you last see this absent parent?

Like I said. He brought Ashley with him of course, and in trailed his mother and father, with a slew of other guests and their gifts. The table was full and it was almost 2:15; the party was barely starting. Almost everyone I knew and even people I'd only had one class with or spoken to once came to my shower.

Henry's smooth babybrown skin and smile projected happiness across his face, as random friends and family walked up to him for hugs,

## MONTH EIGHT: ABSENT PARENT QUESTIONNAIRE

unaware of our status. Our nonexistent now-stranger status. Every time someone congratulated him, baby Henry flipped in my stomach.

I looked over at Henry. His eyes were glossy and flickering around the room as if scanning all of his enemies. Soon there would be a red laser and things would start blowing up.

## 10. Where does the absent parent live now?

He lives in Hopeless, California, with his parents. Which probably isn't conducive to our future together because he doesn't have his own house or car. What was I thinking? What am I doing?

## MONTH EIGHT: ABSENT PARENT QUESTIONNAIRE

Henry coming to my baby shower after not speaking to me throughout all of my pregnancy is like trying to put out the fire in hell with a fan. Mama invited him and his family. She thought it was the "adult thing to do."

I am thinking about how I drove my mom to work in Beverly Hills, and then I drove myself to school as usual. I am thinking about how I plan to go to school up until the second I give birth, maybe even while I am having contractions, and I am thinking that if I do things this way, I will still be able to graduate on time.

I am thinking about the house Henry lives in and squinting to remember how I'd visited once or twice, when Roxanne begins the first game at my shower with cotton balls all over the floor, a big kitchen spoon, and two large bowls. While she explains the game

## MONTH EIGHT: ABSENT PARENT QUESTIONNAIRE

to an audience of at least fifty-nine talking people, Henry walks over—once again staring at my very ready belly.

"So how you been?"

"Pregnant." I'd like to reach around his throat and choke him slowly.

"Yeah, uh, I know that, but like how you been, other than that?"

"Does it matter to you, or are you just making small talk?"

"It matters to me, and I'm making small talk."

## MONTH EIGHT: ABSENT PARENT QUESTIONNAIRE

"I've been ok. I'm getting fat."

A pause of silence and air, a nod.

"So, you gonna be around for the baby when he gets here, Henry? 'Cause so far, you've been ghost."

"Yeh, nah, I mean I've been going through a lot, but I wanted to tell you I'm going to start being around for him."

"Alright, well, you're welcome anytime… just don't tell me you're going to be around and then disappear because that's the part that gets me. If you aren't, just don't, but don't say you will and then change your mind."

## MONTH EIGHT: ABSENT PARENT QUESTIONNAIRE

I pause.

"I mean, I can take a lot, Henry, but I can't take you making promises you can't keep. I can't take that at all. I'd rather you just say you aren't gonna be there."

"Naw, naw, I got you. I'll be there, from now on, I'll be there."

## 11. What is the last known complete address of the absentee parent?

123 N. Western St.

Hopeless, CA 12345

## MONTH EIGHT: ABSENT PARENT QUESTIONNAIRE

## 12. Does the absent parent have a mailing address different from the address above, or a previous address?

I wouldn't know that.

## 13. How long have you known the absent parent?

One year. I made him wait a year for my virginity. We became great friends. Unfortunately, that was either not long enough or not short enough to keep him happy. Or I was not fortunate enough to have been his one and only in our ripe age of promiscuous promises and pisstivities. *Pisstivities* being what my dad used to called activities you engaged in that you had to but didn't want to do. They presumably pissed you off to do them as well. Can you

## MONTH EIGHT: ABSENT PARENT QUESTIONNAIRE

ever really know someone in a year? Can you ever really know someone, at all?

### 14. What kind of work does the absent parent do?

He's a spoiled rotten hopeless romantic in a class clown suit.

### 15. Do you know where the absent parent works now? If yes, what is the employer's name and address?

He's a teenager. He doesn't work, his parents work.

### 16. Do you know where the absent parent previously worked? What was the employer's name and address? Telephone number?

## MONTH EIGHT: ABSENT PARENT QUESTIONNAIRE

Look, he doesn't have a job, he hasn't ever had one to my knowledge, and does this help me with any money for my child? I don't know all of the answers to these questions. I know very little about the subjects here.

**17. Does the absent parent provide medical insurance coverage for you and/or his child(ren)? If yes, insurance company name/policy number/who is covered?**

I don't know if he has a policy number or medical coverage for himself or if he ever will.

**18. What is the absent parent's father's name?**

## MONTH EIGHT: ABSENT PARENT
## QUESTIONNAIRE

(Henry is skimming my baby shower for familiar faces. I can tell.)

Henry Walter Black Sr., I guess. Henry's dad was a pushover; he was tall and chocolate milk–brown colored and looked like a mailman. Henry's mom, Shiree, ordered Henry Sr. around like Pinocchio. You could see his nose growing as he lied to her, trying to keep her happy. I found it amusing, but she didn't have a pleaseable personality. No one was ever going to successfully make her happy, but Henry Sr. seemed to be fine with appeasing her at least.

I remember being appeased. When Henry and I were six months into our relationship, I remember looking at the day in my diary. He appeased me by saying he didn't believe in abortion and if I

MONTH EIGHT: ABSENT PARENT

QUESTIONNAIRE

were to ever get pregnant, he would do everything he could to support me and our baby. I look over at him now, sitting at my baby shower, and study his pretend smile.

When I found out I was pregnant, I thought maybe Henry would marry me like he'd said. Maybe his parents and my parents would support us. Although getting married young wasn't a plan I had, it was always an option I wanted if something like this were to happen. Maybe I should have just gotten the fucking abortion. If I had, I would not be here pretending to celebrate, looking at Henry's parents, people I not only don't want to be around but don't want to know.

## 19. What is the absent parent's mother's name?

Shiree Golter-Black.

## MONTH EIGHT: ABSENT PARENT
## QUESTIONNAIRE

It's only because I'd heard Henry use her maiden name that I know it is Golter. When I first went to Henry's house, his mother had light brownish-blond hair, and I thought they were rich because they had bright white carpet that was not dingy and still held vacuum marks, and she kept calling to Henry to have his friends stay off her carpet and get away from her damn crystal. She was a bright yellow-beige complexion with smooth skin like her son. She had a snippy attitude that made everyone around her feel like she thought she was better off than they were, and she spoke to me like I was below her by flippantly brushing her hand in my face and speaking at me too slowly, like I was heard of hearing.

## MONTH EIGHT: ABSENT PARENT

## QUESTIONNAIRE

## 20. Name and place of court?

Los Angeles? Yeah, that's right, Court of Los Angeles. But currently I'm at my baby shower wishing I didn't have to recall filling out this paperwork.

## 21. Is the absent parent supposed to provide child support under a court order?

No, not yet, but hopefully. That way he'll at least end up having to pay in some way shape or form. I mean, c'mon. There comes a time I should stop being afraid for what he must be feeling right now and be mindful of what's going to happen to me and my son. It's about time I stop being foolish and think about myself. It's about time I see if he will pay some child support. The baby will be here soon enough, and he hasn't done anything else. I am going

## MONTH EIGHT: ABSENT PARENT QUESTIONNAIRE

to have to go through this horrific and unfortunate self-inflicted pain thinking this dumb young boy loved me, and then I'm going to have to figure out how to raise our son alone—without a career path in place, or money for when he needs anything, and without Henry's emotional support. I would be a damn fool to worry about him coming back now. So if he's not ever coming back, who cares if he's "in the system" like everyone else?

## 22. Have you and the absent parent ever been to court for any reason?

Nope, but he's been in trouble before. He's stolen cars, clothes, shoes, and all kinds of stuff. But he never did that stuff when we were together. He wore his uniform, he made Bs, and he spoke like rain was going to fall if he asked.

## MONTH EIGHT: ABSENT PARENT QUESTIONNAIRE

## 23. What is the absent parent's date of birth?

Well, that's easy: December. Henry was born on the fourteenth of December. A Sagittarius, stubborn as ever. Just like my son will be if he's born in December—oh no, my son will be a Sagittarius as well. *Go figure.*

## 24. Where was the absent parent born?

Absent parent? Yea, he's absent all right, he's absent in his mind right now. I guess he was born in Los Angeles.

## 25. Where does he/she live?

In Hopeless, CA somewhere, by the Mobil station, or was that a Chevron? Or no, no, it's a teriyaki restaurant.

## MONTH EIGHT: ABSENT PARENT QUESTIONNAIRE

### 26. What is his/her telephone number?

(213) 755-1234

### 27. How do you contact the absent parent during an emergency?

I wouldn't know. He won't even call me back when it's not an emergency.

### 28. Is the absent parent working?

Working my damn nerves.

### 29. Where did he/she used to work?

## MONTH EIGHT: ABSENT PARENT QUESTIONNAIRE

Henry has never held a job as far as I know. His parents used to give him money, and when they stopped giving him money, he started stealing.

In the middle of this party, I look over at Henry raiding the punch bowl and grabbing the trail mix. My friends are mingling with the boy who has become my enemy. I want to tell them to stay away from him before they get a dose of dumb and end up pregnant too.

## 30. Does the absent parent have work-related income?

Didn't I answer this question already?

MONTH EIGHT: ABSENT PARENT QUESTIONNAIRE

**31. Has the absent parent voluntarily given you child support money (without a court order)? If yes, provide the information requested below and bring a copy of the court order to the interview.**

Nah, he hasn't given me "a pot to piss in or a window to throw it out of."

**Directly to you: Amount $0.00      per: Never**

**For which child(ren)?**

I'm not ever having any more children. This is enough for my entire life.

**32. Date last received:**

## MONTH EIGHT: ABSENT PARENT QUESTIONNAIRE

I have never received any funds from Henry, his parents, or anyone else. That is why I am filling out this form—because I need money.

The game ends in slow motion for me as my Aunt Ruby, blindfolded and down on her knees, scoops a pile of air into another empty bowl of air. The audience is cheering her on, and some people holler out, "Keep going, just a little more!" Aunt Ruby takes her blindfold off only to find both of her buckets empty, probably due to her not holding her bowl straight when the timer initially started. Panic makes people react foolishly. If she had taken her time, she would have remembered where the cotton balls were, she would have had at least a few cotton balls in her bowl, and she would have kept her bowl upright so that none of the

## MONTH EIGHT: ABSENT PARENT QUESTIONNAIRE

cotton balls she caught would have fallen out. She wasn't thinking. And Henry wasn't either. But for once, I am.

Roxanne passes around a jar of jelly beans and collects everyone's estimations of how many are in the jar. Roxanne looks like me, but she's a tad older, with heavy breasts and wider hips. Her mouth is as loud as my sister, who is screaming out impossible number guesses as everyone laughs.

Ia grabs paper and pens and advises everyone to write down possible baby names that consist of the letters in the mother and father's names. Henry and Lalanii. I no longer like the sound of those two names together. People guess,

"Larry!"

## MONTH EIGHT: ABSENT PARENT QUESTIONNAIRE

"Ray!"

More names come about, but none to my liking.

My cousin Wanda has set the table full of ten "dirty diapers." The "poop" is baby food spread on the bottom of the diaper, and each guest takes turns smelling the insides of the diapers, attempting to guess the flavor of the baby food. I can't stop staring at Henry.

The kids under twelve are winning at the clothespin game because most of the adults keep either crossing their arms or legs or mistakenly saying "baby." My stomach is growling again as the game ends.

I am happy enough when cake time comes, but the photo opportunities are miserable as Henry and I stumble through

## MONTH EIGHT: ABSENT PARENT QUESTIONNAIRE

awkward moments of our nonrelationship, uncertain about the way we should behave toward each other at this point. Every time he looks at me, I can see the reflection of my double chin bouncing off the clear window against the balloons fidgeting in the recreation room. My eyes swell up, but I will not let out one tear. I hate the way I look and vow to never secretly judge overweight people again. I'm unhappy it's all a charade, it's all pretending, it's as fake as Henry's love for me had been. I am dying for this to be over.

## 33. Does the absent parent have a driver's license? If yes, in which state? Specify: Year and state?

Henry could drive, he liked to profess to the world, although wherever we went, Ashley or one of my other friends had to drive

## MONTH EIGHT: ABSENT PARENT
## QUESTIONNAIRE

us. Henry didn't have a license at that time and definitely wasn't responsible enough at home for his parents to let him get a permit.

It's time for food. I do know everyone loves Mama's spaghetti; it is always splendid. Roxanne, Wanda, and Ia all grab the French bread, salad dressings, and more eating utensils from the kitchen. My godmom (one of my favorite people) walks up to me.

> "And how's my favorite godchild?"

> "Just fine, Nanny, how are you?"

> "Oh, same ole, same ole… no news is good news. You excited?"

## MONTH EIGHT: ABSENT PARENT QUESTIONNAIRE

"I'm scared, I'm impatient, I'm ready to get this over with so I can meet my son."

"I know that's right, honey! And you know me and your godfather will be right here, every step of the way, anything you need. We got you that bundle of diapers over there, and any time you run low, you just call and I will bring you more."

"Ok, Nanny, I love you, thank you!"

I stare out over at the stack of diapers—taller than me, probably enough cases to last until he's six! Tears well up again.

MONTH EIGHT: ABSENT PARENT

QUESTIONNAIRE

## 34. Does the absent parent have any of the following: tattoos or defining body marks?

My sister's gargantuan laughter takes over the place. She calls everybody to sit in a semicircle and everyone scatters, then gathers.

Henry doesn't have any tattoos. I am staring at the middle of his collared shirt because I am trying to see through it in order to remember any marks, but all I am coming up with are flashes from our second naked encounter:

Martha was home with me, and Daddy was in the process of moving his business from his office. He could no longer afford the overhead for both the house and the office since business was slowing down. He was talking about retirement.

## MONTH EIGHT: ABSENT PARENT QUESTIONNAIRE

Nia had given me pointers on how to keep Henry happy. I couldn't just sleep with him once; I had to keep having sex with him or else he would get it elsewhere or get bored with me. I wasn't crazy about the idea, but I was sure I wasn't going to be remembered as the girl who gave up her virginity in tears. I would be the one and only person Henry had sex with, the last, and the most satisfying for him. Nia explained it would eventually start to feel better for me. She told me I should shower and purposely forget to get dressed. If I answered the door in just my towel, Henry would feel the excitement and know what to do from there. I knew that because Henry and I were comfortable kissing, and the fact that we'd already had sex once and talked about it over the phone quite often, he'd be ok with it again.

## MONTH EIGHT: ABSENT PARENT
## QUESTIONNAIRE

I answered the door wrapped in a faded light-green towel, still partially wet. Martha was singing something no other person could understand as she swept the back steps. I knew if Henry went into my room quickly, she wouldn't see. I opened the door with my fingertip to my mouth to be sure Henry knew to be quiet. He followed me down the white-carpeted hallway that had no pictures on the walls. If Mama had still lived there, she would have had pictures.

As I walked Henry back to my bedroom, I wished Mama still lived with us. I think I was almost fourteen when we moved from the house I grew up in to this one. This house, I knew, was haunted. The old lady who'd lived here before was a wreck in concentric circles, and the neighborhood boys had been sure to tell me about

## MONTH EIGHT: ABSENT PARENT
## QUESTIONNAIRE

her and how she sometimes did voodoo-like magic in the attic. I hardly ever slept in the room, and I often had nightmares about her.

Inside of my room, it was warm. Pink and blue sheer drapes covered the one window. Stale incense and dust swarmed in the air. My furniture was an all-white daybed, a tiny sliding door closet, a large white dresser, a side table, and a black cart that held a big round-bellied television. I kept two floor heaters on at all times, and my twin bed was made up with teddy bears and a purple-and-white blanket with swirls or flowers. Henry came in wearing an oversized white shirt, light blue jeans, and whatever the newest Jordan shoe was. He put a lot of effort into his clothes being pressed every morning, while I purposely looked for clothes that never had to be ironed.

## MONTH EIGHT: ABSENT PARENT QUESTIONNAIRE

He was playfully grabbing at me and I had my towel tucked tightly while fiddling with my hair, trying to make it seem longer than it was. When we got into my room, Henry sat on the bed, and I searched the floor for my favorite blue brush. I found it hiding under a pile of laundry, and as I bent over to grab it, my towel fell to the floor. I stared at him. I stood in an awkward wordlessness as we both scrambled to figure out what to do with our awe. I attempted to pick up my towel, but his eyes were stuck on my naked body—I knew the damage had already been done. When we'd initially slept together, it was dark and mucky and there wasn't much to be seen, only felt. I unconsciously grabbed at my towel, unable to pick it up as it had fallen a bit farther away from me than I realized. My eyes were stuck on Henry and his reaction. His face looked like he'd seen a ghost, not a person, not naked but levitating.

## MONTH EIGHT: ABSENT PARENT QUESTIONNAIRE

I grabbed at the floor for what seemed like forever and self-consciously rushed toward the bed where Henry sat. He reached over and started whispering as he held my head in his large hands. He started talking about school or basketball when I leaned over to smell his neck.

"Are you smelling me?"

"Yep!" I said with all the confidence I didn't have.

"I miss you a very lot," Henry said, and I giggled.

It had been a few weeks since we'd last seen each other, and it was getting harder and harder for him to beg Ashley to pick him up and drop him off every time he wanted to see me. Ashley had gotten a

## MONTH EIGHT: ABSENT PARENT
## QUESTIONNAIRE

girlfriend named Stephanie, who I'd known because she hung out with my friend Nia. Ashley and Stephanie had their own agenda, and it did not involve toting Henry and I around. Henry took his shoes off, and the bed squeaked at his body weight. We hugged long enough for it to feel unnatural, and I kissed his neck. I again kissed up the side of his neck and felt him kissing me back. When Mama would see me with the cordless phone glued to my ear, she would say, "There ain't that much fuckin' shit to talk about in the whole worldddd." I thought about this as I squeezed Henry's neck. I thought about the fact that no one could keep us from each other.

Henry raised his shirt up, over, and off as I walked to the door to lock it from the inside. When I looked over, his body was rippled and lean, not like a body builder but like an active teenage boy. I

## MONTH EIGHT: ABSENT PARENT

## QUESTIONNAIRE

began kissing his collarbone, and soon I let my towel fall off, not an ounce of insecurity left. I felt him kissing my breasts one by one slowly, and it actually felt relaxing, which was shocking. He reached his hand between my legs and slowly pressed his hands in my warmth, and I impulsively moaned. He kissed me again to keep me quiet. When his hands moved, I could feel my own wetness. He lay over me naked as a bird, and when I closed my eyes it was the first time I saw his wings. I'd never been so comfortable with myself in my life.

I felt him fiddle around near his pants and pull up a condom. He struggled with it, making an ugly face, and I began to get nervous. When he had the condom on, he pressed into my skin with a jerking motion that scared me. He stopped to kiss me, and I whispered,

## MONTH EIGHT: ABSENT PARENT QUESTIONNAIRE

"Wait, wait, wait…"

"What, what's up?"

"I dunno, I'm nervous, I—just, just wait."

Henry waited impatiently as I lay there, holding my arms around his neck for at least three minutes. I took a deep breath and this time, I forced my body into his hardness and ignored the scathing pain as much as I could. I felt him moving inside of me, and although he started to move more smoothly, the pain was still unsettling. I was so nervous I didn't realize I wasn't as wet anymore.

I felt him start to scurry faster inside of me, and with each stroke I clenched my teeth together. He wasn't caressing my breasts

## MONTH EIGHT: ABSENT PARENT QUESTIONNAIRE

anymore, but I decided to ignore it and try to kiss him. I forced my legs to open wider, and he began to move inside with ease. It started to hurt less but was still uncomfortable. I had to keep kissing him to remind him I was there. He kept raging in me back and forth, and there were no words in my body to say anything, especially not *stop*.

It looked as though he was staring at the door in concentration for a while as he gained momentum like he was in some robotic race. In and out like a schizophrenic rabid dog. He jackhammered inside of me, without any whispering to me, without any *it's ok*'s, as he had done before. He jammed in and smashed deeper every few thrusts enough to finally make me cry out. It was too hard. At last it was too much for me to endure, and I screamed,

## MONTH EIGHT: ABSENT PARENT

## QUESTIONNAIRE

"Ok, ok, ok, stop."

But he was too far gone.

His arms and back undid the arch, and his body went limp with his face pressed into my chest. He quickly came out of me and kissed the side of my face while grabbing his boxers. He threw the condom into the wastebasket in the corner of the room and began getting dressed. I sat there in shock, taking in the throbbing and aching, feeling a heartbeat between my legs. We both widened our eyes together as we heard the side door slam, signaling my father's arrival. I grabbed the phone to call my friend Esther to make sure she was still making her way over later, and she said she was on her way now. Henry and I finished getting dressed, figuring we could sneak him out of the window once Esther arrived; we were pretty loud as giggling girls.

## MONTH EIGHT: ABSENT PARENT
## QUESTIONNAIRE

I couldn't shake how used I felt. This was not him. He was so different. So different so quickly.

When Esther arrived, she immediately sensed the tenseness. She said it smelled like a window should be opened. When I closed the door, Henry nonchalantly hopped out of the closet. Everyone fell out in laughter as they greeted each other. Esther had gotten her tongue pierced at the beach that day without her parents noticing. She was a temptress, which contrasted with her biblical name. Her petite figure was flawless, with the top of her Guess jeans folded over as she swished with Gly-Oxide to prevent infection of the new piercing. She held her dark hair to one shoulder and leaned over the wastebasket to spit and screamed, "Oh my Gooooood, what is that doing in there? It's a condom in the trashcan! What the fuck?"

## MONTH EIGHT: ABSENT PARENT QUESTIONNAIRE

Henry and I *sssshhh*ed her as we laughed, and I scolded Henry for not wrapping it in a tissue first. We wait for her older boyfriend to come to take us to the movies in his Bronco. Esther said he might bring a friend for me, but I couldn't do anything but think about Henry and what had just happened. She told my dad it was her brother's friend who would chaperone us. My dad believed anything that came out of her innocent little face. Henry waited at the corner up from my house for Ashley to arrive.

At the movies, I got nauseous. Within the next week, Henry forgot to call me back a few times, which was out of character. Less than a week later, I found out that I was seven weeks pregnant. This meant that I'd gotten pregnant the first time Henry and I had sex, just as he was beginning to lose interest.

MONTH EIGHT: ABSENT PARENT QUESTIONNAIRE

## 35. Has the absent parent ever voluntarily paid tuition or school expenses?

I wake up from this flash with my sister wailing,

> "Everybody, we gonna open the presents for Twiggi and her new baby!"

I am absolutely mortified as she repeats my childhood nickname. Some of my high school friends are commenting, some of my closest friends are off and away eating, starting to pay attention. Nia is standing next to me, constantly rubbing on my belly, asking if I feel ok or need to get off my feet.

> "I'm fine, Nia, but just look at *him*."

## MONTH EIGHT: ABSENT PARENT

## QUESTIONNAIRE

Henry is carrying on nonchalantly, without a worry and not much concerned about the future, which infuriates me.

> "Girl, leave that man to be. He hasn't been here, he isn't gonna start being here just because he says so or you hope so. Let that man do him, and you do *you*."

> "It's just so frustrating, I didn't make this child by myself, and yet everything I do from this point forward will be with my child alone. I never meant for this to happen."

My voice creaks at the end as I scoot to sit next to Henry front center stage where everyone is urging me to be next to him. I hardly want to touch the boy. To smile and take fake pictures when soon he's going to be nothing but a memory.

## MONTH EIGHT: ABSENT PARENT QUESTIONNAIRE

## 36. What are the names and addresses of the absent parent's relatives and friends?

I can't remember any of his friends or relatives. I don't care. My cousin Ia writes down what gift is from whom, and halfway through I start to feel tired. Henry begins to help to open gifts as well as reading the cards. From every gift, Roxanne keeps the packaging or bow and decorates two paper plates using the bows, ribbons, tape, and decorations from each gift box. She constructs a ridiculous hat out of it and has us smile for a photo. Henry put his arm around me like a pal, and my whole body wants to deflate. My face flushes red, my blood runs faster in my veins, faster. I can feel rocks and dry grain in my throat. We both turn our heads in toward

## MONTH EIGHT: ABSENT PARENT QUESTIONNAIRE

each other, like newlyweds who just created the most beautiful baby they've been wanting for years.

Henry's parents sit excluded from everyone else, but together. I look over and wish that my parents were at my baby shower together, that my daddy were here, that I was getting married first, that I'd finished school and had some job so no one had to look at me like a "poor little-pregnant-helpless." His family eats, and they compliment Mama on the food, my cousins on the decorations. I can tell they're mumbling things about me, and I glare at them unconsciously.

## MONTH EIGHT: ABSENT PARENT QUESTIONNAIRE

## 37. Are there special health expenses for the absent parent's child(ren)?

I worry about whether my son will be healthy. Who will take care of him if he isn't? Looks like it's all on me. At this point, I am certain he'll never be someone my son can depend on.

## 38. Does the absent parent have any of the following? A car, truck, motorcycle, boat, house, or vacation home?

I don't know if Henry has boats or trucks, and it's very unlikely he owns a vacation home unless he's stealing from it, or smoking in it, which is possible from what I've heard lately. But he and his

## MONTH EIGHT: ABSENT PARENT QUESTIONNAIRE

parents were at my baby shower bearing gifts I pretended to not be impressed by.

I sent my dad an invitation. He didn't come.

I think about how embarrassing it was at the welfare office. All of these questions I don't know and probably will never know and how much I realize I don't know about the father of the baby I am carrying. How hypersonic the last few months have been, how overwhelming, and how often my "baby daddy" doesn't think about what it is like to become a dad.

People start cutting lemon cake. The conversation flips to Carol, who made the cakes. Roxanne announces to everyone,

## MONTH EIGHT: ABSENT PARENT QUESTIONNAIRE

"Y'all don't have to go home… but y'all do have to get the hell up outta here!"

I fake-laugh to end the day faster, and now I'm happy. I'm now very excited to go upstairs away from all of these people who just want to stare at me. I'm really excited, really, really excited to be left alone to think and to open every gift for my son. And prepare.

**I certify that the above statements are correct to the best of my knowledge.**

*Lalanii Rochelle Grant*

---

# MONTH NINE:

# LABOR

"I'M GOING TO DIE"

MONTH NINE: LABOR

## ACT ONE

### SCENE A: IT'S A SLIPPERY HOPELESS

FADE IN:

### TITLE CARD: "I'M GOING TO DIE"

ext. CULVER PARK CONTINUATION - AFTERNOON -

The office is located at the front of the school, facing the entrance. It is colored a dreary blue with shades of gray. Trees surround the left side of the school, opening to a park.

Establishing shot pans down, revealing Lalanii duck-waddling then waving and calling

## MONTH NINE: LABOR

as she passes through the front office. Only teachers are allowed to enter and exit, but she's gotten so close to the staff, they don't mind her.

> I'm never upset from the outside. I often strike up conversations with strangers, and I eat lunch in Tatiana's room while I read her my poetry every day.
>
> Tati's class leaves their journals in a cardboard box overnight for commentary on their writing. My journal is pretty much full of anxiety-ridden poetry.

Lalanii walks toward the camera from a distance. The camera jumps documentary-style as her high ponytail of curls flops against her fat cheeks. She wears a white T-shirt and her favorite pair of beige oversized

## MONTH NINE: LABOR

maternity overalls, and she resembles a farm
worker who eats everything on the farm.

As the camera gets closer, Lalanii flees the
front door, holding her purse, her backpack,
and the Sandra Cisneros book Tatiana has
assigned for reading.

> "See you tomorrow, Lalanii," the front receptionist says.

> "See you tomorrow!"

Lalanii's foot misses the second stair. She
fumbles, but it's too late. She falls forward
hard onto her belly so quickly she's unable
to catch herself. Lalanii says between heavy
pants:

> "Oh my God somebody oH my god!"

MONTH NINE: LABOR

((AS A CROWD GROWS AROUND HER))

"Are you ok, Lalanii?"

((SCREAMS AND QUESTIONS FROM OTHER STUDENTS - MUFFLED))

"Are you ok?"

"Is the baby ok?"

"Do you want me to call the doctor?"

"I don't know, I don't know," I mumble incoherently.

Lalanii leans over to her side, clutching her overlarge belly tightly. Wincing. The camera

## MONTH NINE: LABOR

zooms to her abdomen (where she clutches her stomach). Her lips quiver.

"Just call my Mama! Just call my Mom!" I yell.

The receptionist rushes to the phone. The passersby sit in silence. Lalanii sobs while rocking on her side.

**FADE SCENE**

MONTH NINE: LABOR

## ACT ONE

## SCENE B: BAGEL BABY

FADE IN:

## TITLE CARD: "AFTER HER FALL"

INT.   CAMEO WOODS CONDOMINIUMS - 7:00 A.M. -

Lalanii wakes up in her own bed. She is sore and feels pain all over. Angry birds rustle at the window. She vaguely recalls her mom speaking to her doctor after her fall. He'd advised her mom to tell her she should take it easy. She hears Mama getting dressed for work.

"Mahhhhhhhhhh!" I call out.

## MONTH NINE: LABOR

"What, Twiggi? I'm right here," Ma blurts back.

"I don't think I feel so good," I say, rubbing my belly and thigh.

Ma poses with her hands on her hips, peering
from the hallway into Lalanii's room. Lalanii
is in bed later than usual.

"You just need to eat sumpthin. Get ya lazy ass up and eat sumpthin. There's bagels in there."

"Not hungry, noOoOo. Bagels sounds nasty. They're prolly not even that good. How long've they been in there?" I say back.

## MONTH NINE: LABOR

"Awh, shit, Twiggi, not that long, now get on up and eat. I gotta get off to this dayum job 'fore them folks up there get ta trippen."

"Ok, love you." I half fake-smile at her.

"Love you too, honey. Getcho ass up now and fix those bagels. Put something good on it, you better feed that lil' boy in there."

Lalanii huffs hard at her mom as she heads off to work. She walks in the kitchen, lazily slamming cabinets, looking for something to put on her bagel. She grabs the cinnamon then the butter and clobbers the bagel with both. She heats the bagel up in the microwave for one minute. She bites into the bagel. Butter and cinnamon ooze down her chin. A bad taste

## MONTH NINE: LABOR

tickles her throat. All of a sudden, a look
of disgust overwhelms her face. She rushes to
the bathroom and leans over the sink and
starts to hurl. As her body thrusts forward,
liquid trickles down her legs. Unable to stop
it, she reaches down below with a piece of
toilet tissue and dabs at her underwear. She
sees there is tinged yellowy ooze and blood
on the tissue. Without pulling her underwear
up, she hobbles to the phone, hand shaking.
The phone goes straight to voicemail. She
dials again. Ma picks up.

> "Mama, I think my water just broke. Come home come home!"

> "Aww shit, Twiggi, not today, laaawd, today. Alright, hun, I'll be there in a second."

## MONTH NINE: LABOR


Lalanii looks around the room, making sure there isn't anything she is forgetting from her already packed teddy bear-shaped bag: Pre-pregnancy jeans she was sure she'd be wearing in just a few hours, deodorant, a teddy bear, a toothbrush, her poetry journal, the diaper bag filled with a teething ring, pacifier, diapers, and seven changes of the nicest, tiniest baby clothes she'd washed after her baby shower.

Very slowly, pressure in her abdomen begins to grow. She rocks through it with slow moans, exaggerating them like in the pregnancy movies. She giggles. She feels like a real adult now. She groans again, making herself laugh as she makes her pain seem even worse than it is.

INT.   INSIDE OF MOM'S GREEN HONDA — 8:00 A.M.-ISH —

## MONTH NINE: LABOR

"Dennng, Mama," I say.

"I know we rollin' ain't we?" Ma turns her head to me, glee spreading across her face.

```
Ma rushes to the hospital. Lalanii pats at
her stomach and whispers to her belly on the
way there. The Honda screeches with vengeance
around the corners.
```

"Ahhhh!" I scream.

"What, honey! You ok? We almost there!" Ma shouts back, a sharp turn again to the steering wheel.

Lalanii bursts into laughter.

## MONTH NINE: LABOR

"You just wait. Shits gon' get real in just a second," Ma retorts.

"Yep, and I am having a natural birth without medication. Watch me." I roll my eyes and wince.

"We'll see."

Ma pulls into the driveway as Lalanii's face begins to spoil into a painful frown. Pressure has turned into contractions. Every few minutes, Lalanii's face is tainted more and more with the growing fear. Lalanii steps out of the car holding her stomach and stares up to the sky like a little girl waiting to cross the street alone for the first time.

EXT. CENTINELA HOSPITAL'S FRONT DOORS - 9:00 A.M. -

## MONTH NINE: LABOR

The hospital is crowded. At first glance, the
monstrous place looks like rows and rows of
windows stacked. The camera pans to focus
through the entrance at the women in the
waiting area, screaming. Low-moaning and
distant hollers you wish would disappear out
of earshot. Lalanii's face saddens as 9:05
approaches. Hunger sets in.

> "I need to check my daughter in."

> "Is she in labor?" the receptionist knows the answer to this question. She's just one of those who follow protocol a bit too precisely. Ma and I look at each other sure this woman will irk us if we see her again too soon.

> "Her water just broke all over the damn place!" Ma shrieks, hands flailing.

MONTH NINE: LABOR

A second nurse interrupts the first to inform Lalanii and her mother that there will be "a bit of a wait" for a bed, as they are "crowded." Whenever someone says "a bit of an" anything, it triggers times when Lalanii has waited *forever.* She sits in the hallway starting to fluster. Mama starts calling everybody she knows.

> "Girl, Twiggi in labor!" Again, my childhood nickname—surely she should know by now how much I've grown to dislike it. She wasn't going to make this a pleasurable experience at all.

A random person screams in pain from inside a room—a shocking reminder of being in a hospital. Muffled background noise no one can make out. Cars roar louder in the distance as the automatic sliding window doors open and

## MONTH NINE: LABOR

then close. A rolling cart gets stuck in a
hole in the ground. A baby whines.

> "Nuh-uhhh, girl, I dunno, yeah she fine, nawww nah not
> yet." Ma continues her conversation like this all isn't
> happening. There's no emergency. Pressure isn't building
> and her leg isn't shaking profusely. The uncontrollable
> urge to "get this over with" overwhelms Lalanii.

Lalanii bites down on her lip and grips the
chair. She recalls the way her father had
gripped the metal chairs in the abortion
clinic, knuckles stubborn with worry. Lalanii
remembers how his face looked as she walked
into the doctor's office intending to come
out drugged from her abortion. Worry-free. It
would have only taken a few minutes, she
thinks. She shakes her head to shake off the

## MONTH NINE: LABOR

thoughts as the camera pans to these memories
then back again.

MONTH NINE: LABOR

## ACT ONE

## SCENE C: DILATION

FADE IN:

## TITLE CARD: "BED'S READY"

INT. CENTINELA HOSPITAL – 10:35 A.M. –

When a bed is available, the nurse calls for Lalanii and her mother to be placed in the room. Lalanii's eyes are teary, and she's fallen entirely silent. Her eyebrows are low, and her delightful fake moaning has turned to a constipated-like whine. The nurse is a heavyset woman with large breasts and fluffy hair. She usually wears glasses, but not right now—there are lines below her eyes. She reminds Lalanii of her sixth grade teacher because she looks like she inspired the

## MONTH NINE: LABOR


creators of Miss Piggy, mostly by the
seemingly flared permanently open nostrils.
She repeatedly mispronounces Lalanii's name:
a different way each time she says it. The
piggy nurse supplies Lalanii with a gown and
tells her to change. The other nurses acts as
though Lalanii doesn't exist.

> "I'm just going to need to check you to see how far
>
> you've dilated," the nurse tells me.
>
> "OooOhh, ok," I moan unpleasantly.

The nurse leans over Lalanii's chest to lay
the bed flat. Lalanii grips the side of the
bed and looks off for her mom, who has
conveniently gone away "for a lil' break"
just right then.

## MONTH NINE: LABOR

"I'm sorry. You'll experience a bit of discomfort," Piggy says.

```
Here they go with this "a bit of" again.
Lalanii leans up, and pressure begins to
pound in her abdomen.
```

```
Lalanii watches as the nurse sticks her hand
below her gown. She feels as the nurse
releases one finger, two, fingers, three
fingers, and then pushes four fingers into
her cervix forcibly. Lalanii screams.
```

"What the fuck?" I roar.

```
Lalanii's reflexes cause her to kick Piggy
between her breasts.
```

```
((PIGGY NURSE DISPLAYS A SHOCKED FACE,
BACKING AWAY SLOWLY))
```

## MONTH NINE: LABOR

Pain washes over Lalanii's face as the camera
pans to her mother walking up.

> "Well, now… how we doin' in here?" An almost smug
> expression on her face and a tone of absolute satisfaction.

> "Your daughter has a potty mouth and won't lie still for
> me to check how far she's dilated. She just kicked me in
> the chest," Piggy tells her.

> "Mama, the big-bellied goat stuck her whole fist inside of
> me and tried to open her hand!"

Piggy nurse walks away, throwing her hands up
in the air. She jabbers off to some of the
other nurses about respect and children
having children.

## MONTH NINE: LABOR

"Now, Twiggi, you can't act like that now. These people are trynna help you."

```
Lalanii rolls her eyes and leans against her
pillow to wait for another contraction.
They're increasing in frequency and strength.
They're getting closer together.
```

"I will need to ask you if you would like to have any medication to ease your pain," says another nurse, short with a forgettable face.

"I'm not taking anything that will hurt my baby."

Then: "AHOOHHh.hhhhhhh.hhhhhh," I moan in excruciating pain.

## MONTH NINE: LABOR


Lalanii leans against the bedpost and tries to breathe. She regrets skipping Lamaze classes for school and work at the art center. Lalanii pouts back in the bed like a child, scrunching her forehead. Lower, heavier moans. Then comes a serious contraction. The camera pans to a close-up as tears build up in her eyes. She blinks them out. She grips the pillow.

MONTH NINE: LABOR

## ACT TWO

## SCENE A: DEMEROL

FADE IN:

## TITLE CARD: "BLEEDING TEARS"

INT.   CENTINELA HOSPITAL - Approx. 11:32 A.M. -


The nurse starts a Demerol drip because she is tired of hearing Lalanii curse like a firecracker. Lalanii falls asleep and is suddenly jerked awake by pain as the nurses urge her to rock and turn over to reposition the baby. She is told the baby is set for a breech birth, which is not an ideal position as it is general for children to be born headfirst.

MONTH NINE: LABOR

"Lalanii, I'm going to need you to turn on your side."

"Auhhhiuuuu." I'm incoherently trying to speak and moan.

Lalanii cries for her mother, her father, and anyone to help her. Her mother stands by helplessly. The look on her face is serious now. Everyone waits.

"Baby, it's ok, babe, it's ok," Ma says.

"Mam-uh, I'm dying. Mom, I'm dying. It hurts so much, I'm dying," I cry back at her.

"You're not dying, love, you're having a baby. Everything's ok. Everything's—"

## MONTH NINE: LABOR

"I am, it just hurts, Mom, it hurts, I'd rather feel anything else, Mom. Tell them I need the epidural." I'm not as tough as I'd hoped for.

"I'll go look for someone." Ma blinks slower at me. Sorry at me and for me.

"Lalanii, it seems we are now too late for any other medication. If you have any medicine at this point, it may adversely affect the health of your baby." The forgettable nurse speaks slowly and lowly.

"Ohhh. Ahhh."

Lalanii drifts off into a medically induced sleep.

MONTH NINE: LABOR

**FADE OUT**

## MONTH NINE: LABOR


INT.   DELIVERY ROOM HOSPITAL – 12:30 P.m. –


Lalanii's mother has disappeared after being advised that delivery could take a few hours. The nurses look at each other, sure Lalanii is ready for delivery, and call for Dr. Nicholas to deliver her baby.

> "AHhhHahahhsuuhhuuuuu!" I scream in a cry.

> "I think it may be time," the forgettable nurse says to Piggy.

Dr. Nicholas enters the scene: a look-alike of Philip Anthony-Rodriguez in *The Secret Life of the American Teenager*. His hair is cut low, almost bald; he has light eyes and smooth almond skin.

MONTH NINE: LABOR

"It looks like we are ready to deliver a baby!" Dr. Nicholas sounds like this is the fun part. I can assure you, it is not.

"Lalanii, we are going to move you to the delivery room so you can start pushing," the forgettable nurse says.

"Not without my mom! Nooo…" I shake my head uncontrollably. Tears again.

The nurses begin moving Lalanii to the delivery room. They begin the womanhunt, searching for her mom on the grounds of the hospital.

MONTH NINE: LABOR

## ACT TWO

## SCENE B: HAVING A BEER

FADE IN:

## TITLE CARD: "IT'S A WHITE BABY!"

INT. DELIVERY ROOM — 12:45 P.M. —

Mom nearly misses the birth after needing to be paged on the intercom. She was out in the back of Centinela Hospital, having a Miller Lite with her lover, Mr. Ze.

Lalanii screams for pain medication in violation of her birth plan while the big-tittied piggy nurse once again informs her of it being too late for that option. Lalanii whimpers.

MONTH NINE: LABOR

"It's time for you to push this baby out, Lalanii," Piggy says sternly.

"I caaaaaan't," I tell her, a long drawl.

"Oh yes—you have no other choice. I need you to push right now." Piggy nurse won't back off.

Lalanii pushes as hard as she can muster and stares off to see a swirl of feces, neat like it had been pushed down by a frozen yogurt nozzle. Her embarrassment fuels tears, and the nurse removes the defecation by pulling at the bed pad. Forgettable nurse encourages her to push again.

Dr. Nicholas gathers his gloves and readies himself for delivery. He advises Lalanii to push steadily and tells her he will tell her

## MONTH NINE: LABOR

to stop pushing so her skin will stretch for
her baby's head to fully crown. Lalanii bears
down while pushing without hearing or
listening to any instruction, and pushes as
hard as she can throughout.

> "I need another hard push just like that, Lalanii," Doc says to me. I hear sounds, not words. I feel meanings. I see blur.
>
> "Uhhhhhhhhhhhhhhhh uuhhhhhhhhh."

Dr. Nicholas finds the head crowning and
advises Lalanii to now stop pushing. As
Lalanii continues to push, the nurses follow
in advisory for her to now hold in the urge
to push.

> "AUUHHHUUUUUUUUUUUUUUUUUUHHH!"

## MONTH NINE: LABOR

I scream in a deep, painful howl, louder than I ever have before. This. Shit. Hurts.

"Do not push anymore, Lalanii! Resist the urge to push or your skin will tear," Dr. Nicholas asserts in a heightened voice.

```
Lalanii hollers as the skin incurs a large
tear as she pushes against the pain to
relieve the pressure of her child. Her skin
tears jaggedly. Camera pans to show a visual
of screams and tears running into her mouth
and down her chin.
```

"Mmmummm… !!"

## MONTH NINE: LABOR

"She's already torn. She'll need a repair. She needs to push once more and get this baby out, now." Forgettable nurse isn't helping.

"Give me one more hard push, Lalanii, and I'll take care of everything else," Dr. Nicholas says strongly, comfortingly.

"AUUHHHHHHHHHHHHHHHHHHHHHHHHHHHH HHHHHHHHHHHHHHHHHHHHHHHHHHHHHHHH HHHHHHHHHHUUUGHUUUUUUUUGHHHGHGHG HGHGH!"

The baby bulges with a slight cry in a blob of red and what appears as white cream. Lalanii whimpers in relief. Dr. Nicholas hands the semibloody baby to his new

## MONTH NINE: LABOR

grandmother to cut the cord with the help of
the other nurse. She reaches to cut the cord
and grab for the baby. Lalanii leans over to
hear her mama.

> ((Singing)) "O youse a cute liddle white babiieeeeee! You are the cutest little whitest babieeee ever! That's my paaaaaapi!" Ma says as she teases him playfully for not having much color in his skin yet.
>
> I hiccup and giggle, then wince in pain.
>
> "Lalanii, I'm going to have to suture. You have a bad tear, and I'll need to stitch the edges of the rectum back together," Dr. Nicholas says straight and firm.

Lalanii moans for a few moments and then
falls back into her bed without first holding

## MONTH NINE: LABOR

her son. When she awakes, she hears her mother having a full conversation with her newborn baby boy, as if he were a ten-year-old. Lalanii looks over at her son and calls him Tye'ler.

MONTH NINE: LABOR

## ACT TWO

## SCENE C: SPERM DONOR

FADE IN:

## TITLE CARD: "WANNA HOLD HIM?"

INT. BEDROOM CENTINELA HOSPITAL –
MIDAFTERNOON –

Among the first of the visitors are Henry and his mother and father. Lalanii hears of Henry's arrival, says hello, and watches as he holds his son in complete awe. Lalanii's mother takes off, explaining that there will be plenty of nurses to take care of Lalanii and her son tonight. She says she will see her in the morning. Henry continues to hold his child for a short while, only looking up once at Lalanii. Lalanii pretends to fall

## MONTH NINE: LABOR

slowly asleep. She listens as Henry's family compares features on the baby to ensure the child is indeed Henry's.

MONTH NINE: LABOR

## ACT THREE

## SCENE A: CLOTTING RAINFOREST

FADE IN:

## TITLE CARD: "BLOODY MASSACRE"

INT. CENTINELA HOSPITAL BATHROOM - NIGHTFALL -

Lalanii discovers she can't leave the hospital without having a bowel movement and the sanitary napkins look like diapers with clamps. Lalanii fearfully presses the emergency button in the bathroom for a nurse, as her first urination after giving birth is a clot of blood and afterbirth, and it stings.

## MONTH NINE: LABOR

"I'm sorry, I'm bleeding and it won't stop, and it's thick and heavy and it comes in big blobs." I'm wailing at her forgettable round face. She's quiet and slow and reassuring. She's nice.

"Yes, hun, it's ok. This will pass. Your body will need some recovery time. But, yes, this amount of blood is normal," the second nurse chimes in from behind her in the doorway.

"It's just so red, and so much. I've just never seen anything—"

((Smiling)) "Yes, all normal. All healthy. You will, however, need to take a number two before being discharged, which won't be fun considering the amount of

## MONTH NINE: LABOR

stitches you've received. I'll go get you some stool softeners to make that process as easy as possible." Piggy nurse has a lot of experience.

"Thank you," I sniffle.

The nice forgettable nurse and Piggy leave the bathroom, and Lalanii looks around, questioning whether or not she should have taken this on at all. Lalanii begins to sob on the toilet, riddled with confusion and fear.

*

Lalanii's body continues to clot and bleed throughout the night. The nurse talks her through the discomfort each time she visits her room. Nice forgettable nurse stands over her and pushes forcefully on her flubbery

## MONTH NINE: LABOR

abdomen while speaking gentle words and
smiling. Lalanii cringes as she feels her
body contracting together and feels the
uncontrollable leakage coming out. The nurse
assures her this is all completely normal.
Lalanii falls into a deep sleep.

MONTH NINE: LABOR

## ACT THREE

## SCENE B: UNINVITED WELL-WISHERS

FADE IN:

## TITLE CARD: "CONGRATULATIONS WHO?"

INT. CENTINELA HOSPITAL ROOM - VISTING HOURS NEXT DAY -

Random numbers of strangers, teachers, students, and family members show up for support, bearing gifts. The space in the room is too small to hold all of the well-wishers.

Lalanii apologizes to and thanks the piggy-nosed nurse and comes to tears when saying good-bye to the nice one the next day.

## MONTH NINE: LABOR

I am in disbelief. I am a mother.

MONTH NINE: LABOR

## ACT THREE

## FINAL SCENE: FEED.IT.

FADE IN:

## TITLE CARD: "HE LOOKS LIKE AN UGLY FISH"

INTERIOR HOSPITAL - LATE EVENING -

> "I have someone who has been looking forward to meeting you," the nice nurse says to me.

She carries the child over to Lalanii. The child is moving his cheeks in a suckling motion, like a fish out of water. Lalanii reaches her hand out nervously and holds her child for the first time.

## MONTH NINE: LABOR


The nurse rolls in a clear bassinet to hold
her baby son. He has blue veins bulging on
his forehead, he is wrinkly and has a lot of
dark, slick hair. He has a very pale-
yellowish complexion. The nurse tells Lalanii
it is common; he has jaundice, and it will
pass. Lalanii thinks he looks uncooked. She
holds him close anyway.

> "What do I do?" I say to her, looking up from him.

> "Feed him," the nice nurse tells me, walking away.

Lalanii's stomach has stretch marks and looks
like cellulite slop. From front to back she
has stitches that need to heal, and she's
told the stitches will then fall out
naturally. The nice nurse says to call her if
she needs anything or has any trouble. She
then leaves her son there for her to
breastfeed. He latches on fine the very first

## MONTH NINE: LABOR

```
time. As he suckles, it is like magic, but
occasionally he stops or slows. Lalanii
places her breast back into his mouth and
touches his cheek. He starts again. He seems
to be getting more color in his face so he is
a vivid yellow; his legs are tiny and
kicking-strong.
```

> Holding him, I sit there and think of what it will mean to be a mother. He is five pounds, six ounces. I watch him quietly fidget for almost an hour, then drift slowly to sleep.
>
> I declare it in the silence. Contentment smiles across my face, by a second sigh, a lot less fear.
>
> This moment is mine. My. Mine. And this baby is mine. And this world is ours. I sigh.

MONTH NINE: LABOR

**FADE OUT**

# EPILOGUE:
# THEY DON'T TELL YOU

They don't tell you that you can't be released from the hospital until after you've had a bowel movement, and that stool softeners after childbirth don't help much when you've been stitched up from vagina to anus. Pregnancy books don't describe the horror when you're waiting to shit. They opt out of a healthy description of the first blaring piss as you sit on the toilet gripping the red-stained diaper-like sanitary napkin at your knees.

Let them not tell you, as you fret for the emergency button in the hospital bathroom, as the nurse speaks to you like you're a slow

## EPILOGUE: THEY DON'T TELL YOU

invalid—assuring you the thick clumps of blood and sloshes of afterbirth will release slowly, no alarm. No alarm as you grip the thick railing with sweaty palms. No alarm as you crave company and the crowds have all gotten over little ole teenage you and her baby, after everyone has gone home—back to their regularly scheduled busy. They're gone and they're no longer worried about you.

As your heart now runs on a battery called motherhood, your little *eek*ing pale-faced baby causes you to cringe every few minutes as you dread his every movement because for babies, every movement makes them cry. Up and up to the bathroom, back and forth. Let your nurse not massage your marshmallow belly, stretched in marks as you feel your stomach gurgle and internal globs tighten and release more blood into your stretch leggings

## EPILOGUE: THEY DON'T TELL YOU

below. As your body tingles with every suckle, your baby boy sips from your breast, you manage a smile.

Tye'ler Julian Grant-Black was born on December 3, 1999. Only hyphenated because you thought it'd be easier to receive child support that way. Except when his father came to visit him at the hospital, he never signed his birth certificate. They also don't tell you that if your son's father only works under the table taking street occupations, you don't receive child support. They don't tell you that if he goes back to jail, in, back out, in again, that the second you get a job and make around a thousand dollars a month—you can no longer get aid from the welfare department. But yet and still, you aren't making that yet, so the $548 you get from welfare and the approximately $300 in food stamps are allowing you to survive.

## EPILOGUE: THEY DON'T TELL YOU

They don't tell you that your son's grandparents might not obligate themselves to their grandchild financially, and they don't tell you that you might have to figure out how to come up with an extra few hundred to pay for his circumcision or for any financial burdens thereafter. You aren't entirely geared up for the sleeplessness and worry. You aren't prepared for wayward check-ins from baby dad's side of the family, only for "show" but always without substantial support.

Arriving home is a whole new ambiance. They don't tell you you'll wear size eleven for a while, after being a size one, and that it's likely you may not ever see your previous size again. They just don't tell you that.

Mama wasn't going for letting me "get comfortable." Tye'ler slept not one night in his crib, and between breastfeedings, my own

## EPILOGUE: THEY DON'T TELL YOU

feedings, loneliness, boredom, and sleepiness, I'd never experienced a more joyless time in my life. I was utterly miserable, and not the postpartum depression the masses warn you about—I'm talking sheer regret. Lack of sleep robs your perception of beauty, and colic cries are a riveting pierce in each day. I was so weakened and exhausted that I could pass out while eating, on the toilet, midsentence, or as I showered, soap bar in hand—no matter.

One night, my body had enough and didn't wake up for his crying. When I opened my eyes, I could see peripherally that Ma had Tye, rocking back and forth down our hallway, singing Minnie Riperton's "Lovin' You. It was my first smile since I'd arrived home. Ma let Tye sleep in her bed that day, and from then on we all slept in her king-size until Tye began sleeping through the

## EPILOGUE: THEY DON'T TELL YOU

night. We'd take turns when my body just wouldn't move, it just took two. It just takes two people to raise a child. Usually more.

In June 2001, I had the grades to transfer from the continuation school back to Culver City High to graduate with my class. The ceremony was on the grass football field outside, and it was a gorgeous afternoon. Tye was an active toddler—bouncing and running. Full of so much personality, he often took his diaper off and gave it to me when it was wet, and he would only fall asleep to breast milk. In the middle of my graduation ceremony, he wriggled from Ma's arms trying to get to me, and as I stepped off the stage after accepting my diploma, the audience cheered for me, red-faced, swooping the toddler up into my arms.

The first guy I dated was when Tye was this age; he was my best friend, and I probably shouldn't have crossed that line. He was a

## EPILOGUE: THEY DON'T TELL YOU

heavyset Hispanic guy I'd gone to school with, and I liked him best because he was "safe." He wasn't the type to break a heart— he was the type to steal immeasurable amounts of candles, teriyaki jerky, and novelties from his job at Trader Joe's and set it up as an altar in my bedroom. I fell in "kindness" with him, not in love. Since I never made my prom, I escorted him to his. We slept together shortly after that night, and the few friends I still had left boasted that he was bragging about me being his girlfriend. I didn't correct it; he was just too sweet. I was also afraid no one else would want me because I had a child. To a certain extent, I was right. Due to the places I went, which were generally the grocery store for ProSobee (a soy-based Enfamil formula) and to the doctor's office, I was unlikely to meet anyone new at all.

## EPILOGUE: THEY DON'T TELL YOU

After one day of meeting no one new, I was distracted and disordered as I pushed Tye in my shopping cart at Albertsons. An obnoxiously loud woman with a bouffant wig-like curly trap on her head exclaimed, "Your little brother is sooooooooooo cute!" Tye cooed and drooled at the attention, and just as I was going to respond, my son smarted off:

"Mammmmmmi, I want tiddy-juice, Mammmmi." The lady sped her cart off, mortified, as I continued on, embarrassed. He'd made this up on his own. His love for juice and all the adults around him referring to my tatas as tiddies—my son said it once and got a reaction, and then, as most parents know, when a child learns something inappropriate, you can't do anything to get them to stop repeating it or doing it. My son would scream, "Tidddddy-juice!" and fall backward onto his head in any store, especially when I was

## EPILOGUE: THEY DON'T TELL YOU

late for something, and often when I was already having a not-so-swell day.

On this day in particular, I needed the necessities, so I was interrupted shortly thereafter by the uncomfortable dread of having to use my food stamps once I reached the counter. The cashier seemed to flail my food stamps around. Luck would glitter me gold that she had to call for change in "food stamps land" over the loudspeaker. The protocol has changed and now there's a fancy food stamp credit card, but when I needed food stamps, they were individual dollar bills. There was no way everyone in line wouldn't know you were so low income you couldn't afford to buy your own food. As she counted each food stamp bill back to me, I squeezed all of my muscles together hoping I could get to Mars that way.

# EPILOGUE: THEY DON'T TELL YOU

**1**

When I got home, I locked myself in my room for a moment to gather my thoughts up neatly. I'd brought up the groceries and put them away, and Ma was folding the towels in the living room and talking on her cell. I left Tye eating his Gerber crackers in the dining room across from the living room. I just needed a second, so I figured it'd be fine to keep my door closed. Ma was cackling, and her voice carried so loudly she could infect the mentally insane with headaches. I had to close my door for just a second. Within moments, Ma had gone down the back steps (cordless phone pinched between her neck and ear) to put another load in, and failed to close the back door.

Tye, wandering without a noise, followed after. What I heard next was a loud boulder-thick thump and a hollowing-holler into a deep

## EPILOGUE: THEY DON'T TELL YOU

unbreathing silence, then a scream from the bottom of the stairs. Tye had gone out after Ma and fallen headfirst down the concrete steps. Blood gushed from his forehead. I don't remember how I flew down the first set of steps, but I swooped him in my arms as close as I could, and Ma squeezed us both together.

"Goddamit, Twiggi, I thought you were watching him!"

"I thought you had him, Ma, he was sitting right next to you!"

We both raced back up the stairs, grabbing a towel. The open skin was white and swollen and cracked slightly, then more blood. Ma wrapped a tiny frozen piece of steak and applied pressure. After twenty minutes, the bleeding lessened. Probably we should have gotten him a few stitches, but I'd given him a cherry Popsicle to stop him from grabbing at me and whimpering. Since I was

## EPILOGUE: THEY DON'T TELL YOU

weaning him from breastfeeding (he was nearly two), it took everything I had not to pop out my breast and serve it to him. I was a machine made for him. I cried myself to sleep holding my son that night. He was just so important that I couldn't have a moment to myself, and it only took one moment.

2

They don't tell you that the physical pain your kids acquire, from falls off the monkey bars or bumps on the coffee table, will heal, but watching your hardly talking toddler wait for his wayward dad while sitting on top of a pillow at the window for hours is an image that will imprint on your mind and inside of your heartbeat and eat at your stomach lining and create the type of slow-boiling hell in the pit of your belly that will take years of counseling to quell—especially when your son's dad doesn't ever show up. Especially

## EPILOGUE: THEY DON'T TELL YOU

when you hear of him bringing two other children into the world. Especially when the child support back pay surpasses $98,000, and you just give up ever pursuing it again. Especially when you hear of him back in and out and back in jail again, but somehow still able to keep an irregularly ignorant contact with your son because it's only fair, right? They don't ever tell you life is fair, so don't you dare believe that.

4

They don't tell you that your little baby's bottom lip will swell up with an infected bump on the inside of it because of the germs he acquired from still sucking his thumb years later—which you'd thought was cute on the ultrasound when he was inside of you but is absolutely most impossibly not as cute when you have to watch your kid count slowly and see his eyes roll back as a doctor puts

## EPILOGUE: THEY DON'T TELL YOU

him to sleep so they can perform surgery to remove the added skin. They don't tell you about your sagging breasts and stomach skin, which you're told won't even go back to normal unless you opt for plastic surgery. They also don't tell you your father will finally start talking to you again, and meet your son—who'll look like a mix between your dad and his dad; so you might not appear to have had anything to do with creation after all. But, in the process babies heal, so your dad will become your very best friend, and all will feel well again. At least for a bit.

**5**

They don't tell you your kid will get suspended at five years old from the "good school" in the affluent neighborhood for throwing scissors at a teacher. They don't tell you they talk back already at this age. They don't tell you that you won't be able to control him

## EPILOGUE: THEY DON'T TELL YOU

or talk sense into him, so you'll end up having to drive him halfway across town to a specialty private school, so your commute will be 1.5 hours every morning and every afternoon for over two years.

**6 - 7**

They don't tell you the low-income programs that help mothers, like Crystal Stairs, will cut you off once you start making a little money. The same with WIC and additional government assistance programs, as they won't allow you to qualify if you make over a certain amount—which most certainly will happen to be exactly one dollar over what you make.

## EPILOGUE: THEY DON'T TELL YOU

**8 - 10**

They don't tell you your kid will still suck his thumb, even at nine years old. People will still judge you. And at only twenty-five, you've not quite hit the age of dating where EVERYONE has kids yet, so when people hear you have one, they'll judge you and not call you back. When you get into anything serious, the guy will cheat and finally confess it didn't work because he wasn't ready to be a "father figure," among other things.

**TEENAGER**

They fail to explain in any parenting books that at fourteen there'll be cursing and high school and from there you're lucky if you can get any teenager to listen to anything. Sure, you may get lucky. I, however, was not.

## EPILOGUE: THEY DON'T TELL YOU

But then there are the sweet moments: When you fall apart because you've been laid off at your big-time copy/production job at Sony (that isn't paying big-time production bucks, mind you, but gives you great experience and a leg-in) and five minutes after you're let go, they let go of your boss who's just let you go… and you experience your first real job loss. Not "end of contract," not "found a better-paying position"… just a total and complete loss when you were hoping to stay forever and you'd met real friends for the first time ever at a job. And then my son walks slowly into my room to see me crying on my bed and gives me a hug and offers up his entire savings of $253 and thinks that will be enough to cover the house expenses. And it makes you sad in a different way, in a way people who are mothers understand. In an impossible way that makes you say, no matter how bad it is or gets, you don't regret a second of what you've become or what you

## EPILOGUE: THEY DON'T TELL YOU

did to get here. Because you've now found someone who will love
you as-is. As you're falling apart at the good parts, as you're
coming undone at the bad parts, as you're sitting still but shaking
and the aches are in your ribs because the job is gone and someone
else has fallen short in your love life and your mother moves away
because you get engaged and it doesn't work out, but her other
daughter offers her a place to stay and so it's off to the East
Coast for her. And for a while you'll feel sad, but you'll learn
that's numbing.

**16**

At sixteen, he'll confess he's secretly smoking weed but would
rarely ever drink, and you'll respond in the same way your mom
did to you—when you did anything less than favorable—that
you'd rather he do everything bad under your roof without hiding

## EPILOGUE: THEY DON'T TELL YOU

it than getting caught elsewhere and getting into more trouble. And he'll take your kindness for weakness and develop a whole habit.

### 17

At seventeen, they say nothing about your child giving up football after years and years of practices and him being a pretty decent running back, but he'll say he's been writing for a few years and he'll become a rapper. Just like that. And what does that mean to me? Well, that I've sacrificed my life to raise a brilliant Hot Cheeto–eating writer, rapper, and artist with lots of potential. And they don't tell you that before that next year he'll have an entire tattooed sleeve (that he's been hiding) on his beautiful sun-kissed skin and several on his neck and hand.

They just don't tell you that.

## EPILOGUE: THEY DON'T TELL YOU

**18**

Between seventeen and eighteen he'll get his first job waiting tables and get a taste of real tips. Serving people is just the beginning, but I can't stress or press him to use his mind or create a skill set that could be marketable in the event that he'll have to "work" for someone to put food on the table. You know, just in case.

Nope, because by this time, he's a full-blown artist. And good at it, at that.

**19**

They don't tell you that you get less control. And by that time you won't want it, but you'll have no choice. At age nineteen, Tye moved out because he and my ex stopped getting along about

## EPILOGUE: THEY DON'T TELL YOU

trivial things. It really was as simple as him taking care of his chores, and my ex felt he should hold up his end of the bargain. Which he should have and could have, but they don't tell you young adults won't want to, and they'll behave like kids but still be technically adults.

What I've learned as a mother repeats with the same things I've now learned as an adult… it's all about the little things. They don't tell you how expensive dental care is, and definitely they don't explain the Invisalign knock-offs you'll still feel obligated to pay for, which become a whole ordeal, and you'll have to make magic with your bills—still—even when you're doing far better financially. Expensive children turn into expensive adults, and it's all expensive, really. Emotionally and financially.

## EPILOGUE: THEY DON'T TELL YOU

They didn't tell me that by the time my kid was twenty, I'd be thirty-six... and I'd feel more like a distant friend or overworked sister than a young mother. They didn't tell me how to raise a proper man, and especially not how to balance that with becoming the proper mother and proper person. And what is proper, anyway?

They didn't tell me my dad would get old and die in the process, and I'd have my worst breakup at that same time, and that guy would steal from me and hide he was hiked up on drugs. They didn't tell me my son would move back home, because well, a child is... forever. They didn't say that—sometimes—with my son moved back in, I'd want him out, <u>but not</u>, and that a lot of times I'd still feel alone.

## EPILOGUE: THEY DON'T TELL YOU

Sometimes that alone would be lonely, but mostly it wouldn't because one thing about going through a lot mostly alone is that it's hard to know when you actually *need* something or someone.

But they don't explain the growth. They don't explain that because I've learned to value me, and in the process I've learned to love myself, that every step, in every way possible, will make me more resilient.

No one ever tells you as an adult, "You're ok." But I'm ok. They didn't tell me the fears don't ever really go away—so I kept waiting for them to go away. They don't. They just change… into something else. That motherhood will give you a tough shell but break your damn heart, and your haters win if you don't get up again.

## EPILOGUE: THEY DON'T TELL YOU

They didn't tell me that years and years later, I'd still compartmentalize my feelings just like an acrostic poem. But by then, I'd also learned to root for myself.

That I'd still think clearer in poetry than in thought. That my art would be more true to who I am—even after all of these years.

They didn't tell me that my fears began as a kid and that even with a "seemingly ok childhood," the nature vs. nurture of it all would prevail, and no one ever knows how much of their own fears and unresolved emotional or mental experiences will show up in their adult lives later. And we're all not getting out alive, and we all won't be unscathed, and we're all just trying to figure it out a little better along the way rather than how we came.

So, no…

## EPILOGUE: THEY DON'T TELL YOU

I don't have the same worries of being alone as I had when I gave birth to my son, but my fears have transitioned into other feelings of concern.

I'm no longer Pregnorant. The experiences I've had have morphed into: How well will my son take hold of his life, and what will happen to him since I won't live forever, and will he learn to budget and plan, and what will he give back? How will he continue our legacy? And they didn't tell me that these are the questions that might keep me up at night sometimes.

They didn't tell me every time he leaves, I'll worry if he'll get caught around the wrong people or make the wrong decisions. I'll worry if I've raised him well enough to even make those good decisions because life is delicate. If he doesn't make the right

## EPILOGUE: THEY DON'T TELL YOU

decisions, I might blame myself, or he might blame me when things in his life go awry.

And they don't tell you about those days when being a mother on top of everything else is too much and tempers are flaring and he'll say whatever he wants, which isn't the best quality to have, but he won't ever be taken advantage of, and some days I'll think about how much of a wow that is and how far I've come. How far we've made it. And ten years after receiving my master's degree, I'll consider going back to school, but this time not for my dad—for me.

And my kid, who I'll always and forever see on the inside as a child but try to see physically as an adult, will release his first mixed tape live to the world on his twenty-first birthday, and I can't contain my joy or absolute terror for what I know is to come.

## EPILOGUE: THEY DON'T TELL YOU

But I would be as *Pregnorant* as ever—all over again—*for him.*

BETTER EVER AFTER...

THE END.

# ACKNOWLEDGMENTS:

Thank you Tye.

God.

Thanks to all of my family and all of my friends.

My Writers Group, my editors, my first readers, and the typos that still slip through the cracks.

To growth and to all of the goodbyes we have to embrace because we have to be braver. There is just no other way to happiness.

I love you.

Lalanii

www.ingramcontent.com/pod-product-compliance
Lightning Source LLC
Chambersburg PA
CBHW070300010526
44108CB00039B/1396